Freedoms of Navigation in the Asia-Pacific Region

The need for freedoms of navigation in regional waters is frequently mentioned in statements from regional forums, but a common understanding of what constitutes a particular freedom of navigation or the relevant law is lacking.

This book discusses how law, politics and strategy intersect to provide different perspectives of freedoms on navigation in the Asia-Pacific region. These freedoms are very important in this distinctively maritime region, but problems arise over interpreting the navigational regimes under the law of the sea, especially with regard to the rights of foreign warships to transit another country's territorial sea without prior notification or authorisation of the coastal state, and with determining the availability of high seas freedoms of navigation and overflight in an exclusive economic zone. The book explores these issues, referring in particular to the position of the main protagonists on these issues in Asian waters – the United States and China – with their strongly opposing views. The book concludes with a discussion of the prospects for either resolving these different perspectives or for developing confidence-building measures that would reduce the risks of maritime incidents.

Providing a comprehensive yet concise overview of the various different factors affecting freedom of navigation, this book will be a valuable resource for those working or studying in the fields of international relations, maritime security and the law of the sea.

Sam Bateman retired from the Royal Australian Navy as a Commodore (one-star) and is now a Professional Research Fellow at the Australian National Centre for Ocean Resources and Security (ANCORS) at the University of Wollongong, Australia.

Routledge Research on the Law of the Sea

Available titles in this series include:

The International Court of Justice in Maritime Disputes
The Case of Chile and Peru
Julio Faundez

Freedoms of Navigation in the Asia-Pacific Region
Strategic, Political and Legal Factors
Sam Bateman

Freedoms of Navigation in the Asia-Pacific Region
Strategic, Political and Legal Factors

Sam Bateman

LONDON AND NEW YORK

First published 2020
by Routledge
2 Park Square, Milton Park, Abingdon, Oxon OX14 4RN

and by Routledge
605 Third Avenue, New York, NY 10017

First issued in paperback 2021

Routledge is an imprint of the Taylor & Francis Group, an informa business

Copyright © 2020 Sam Bateman

The right of Sam Bateman to be identified as author of this work has been asserted by him in accordance with sections 77 and 78 of the Copyright, Designs and Patents Act 1988.

All rights reserved. No part of this book may be reprinted or reproduced or utilised in any form or by any electronic, mechanical, or other means, now known or hereafter invented, including photocopying and recording, or in any information storage or retrieval system, without permission in writing from the publishers.

Trademark notice: Product or corporate names may be trademarks or registered trademarks, and are used only for identification and explanation without intent to infringe.

Publisher's Note
The publisher has gone to great lengths to ensure the quality of this reprint but points out that some imperfections in the original copies may be apparent.

British Library Cataloguing-in-Publication Data
A catalogue record for this book is available from the British Library

Library of Congress Cataloging-in-Publication Data
Names: Bateman, W. S. G. (Walter Samuel Grono), author.
Title: Freedoms of navigation in the Asia-Pacific region : strategic, political and legal factors / Sam Bateman.
Description: Abingdon, Oxon ; New York, NY : Routledge, 2020. | Series: Routledge research on the law of the sea | Includes bibliographical references and index.
Identifiers: LCCN 2019028243 (print) | LCCN 2019028244 (ebook) | ISBN 9780367189730 (hardback) | ISBN 9780429199585 (ebook)
Subjects: LCSH: Freedom of the seas–East Asia. | Freedom of the seas–Southeast Asia.
Classification: LCC KZA1693.3.B38 2020 (print) | LCC KZA1693.3 (ebook) | DDC 341.4/5091647–dc23
LC record available at https://lccn.loc.gov/2019028243
LC ebook record available at https://lccn.loc.gov/2019028244

ISBN 13: 978-1-03-224040-4 (pbk)
ISBN 13: 978-0-367-18973-0 (hbk)

Typeset in Times New Roman
by Wearset Ltd, Boldon, Tyne and Wear

Contents

List of illustrations   vii
Author's biography   viii
Preface   ix
Acknowledgements   xiii
List of abbreviations   xiv

1 Introduction   1

Introduction 1
Setting the scene 3
Special features 7
Sovereignty disputes 10
Development of the freedoms of navigation 13
Freedoms of navigation in East Asia 16
Outline 20

2 Navigational regimes   25

Innocent passage 25
Transit passage 30
Archipelagic sea lanes passage 37
Normal mode of transit 44
Conclusion 46

3 Exclusive economic zone issues   55

Introduction 55
Development of the EEZ regime 55

The EEZ as international waters 59
Vexed issues 60
Way forward 69

4   Building understandings and confidence   76

Different perspectives 76
Conflicting maritime strategies 77
Maritime confidence-building measures 78
Ambiguities and uncertainties 81
US Freedom of Navigation Program 83
Conclusions 90
Final thoughts 94

Index   100

Illustrations

Table

1.1	Maritime zones of East Asia	6

Figures

1.1	Maritime geography of East Asia	5
2.1	Territorial sea straight baselines of Vietnam	31
2.2	Indonesia's archipelagic sea lanes	40
2.3	Possible Philippine archipelagic sea lanes	42
3.1	EEZs in the Western and Central Pacific	68
4.1	FONOPs in the Paracel Islands	87

Author's biography

Dr Sam Bateman retired from the Royal Australian Navy in 1994 as a Commodore (one-star) and is now a Professorial Research Fellow at the Australian National Centre for Ocean Resources and Security (ANCORS) at the University of Wollongong in Australia, and until 2018, was also an Adviser to the Maritime Security Programme at the S. Rajaratnam School of International Studies (RSIS) at the Nanyang Technological University in Singapore. His naval service included four ship commands ranging from a patrol boat to guided-missile destroyer, as well as several senior postings in the strategic policy and force development areas of the Australian Department of Defence in Canberra, including at one stage being responsible for developing defence policy on the law of the sea. He has written extensively on defence and maritime issues in Australia, the Asia-Pacific and Indian Ocean. He was awarded his PhD by the University of New South Wales in 2001 for a dissertation on 'The Strategic and Political Aspects of the Law of the Sea in East Asian Seas'. His current research interests include regional maritime security, piracy and maritime terrorism, oceans policy, the strategic and political implications of the Law of the Sea, and maritime cooperation and confidence-building. Over the years, he has been involved in numerous Track 1.5 and Track 2 activities relevant to the subject matter of this book. He was for many years co-chair of successive maritime cooperation working groups established by the Council for Security Cooperation in the Asia Pacific (CSCAP). In 2016–2017 he co-chaired a working group of the ASEAN Regional Forum (ARF) Expert and Eminent Persons' (EEPs) Group that conducted a study of lessons learnt and best practice with regard to preventing and managing incidents at sea in the Asia-Pacific region.

Preface

I have been privileged to have been associated with developments in the region with maritime cooperation, maritime confidence building and the law of the sea over the past three decades. Through the 1980s I held several positions in the strategic policy areas of the Australian Department of Defence in Canberra. A posting in the Strategic and International Policy Division 1982–1984 coincided with the finalisation and opening for signature of the 1982 UN Convention on the Law of the Sea (UNCLOS). My responsibilities then included development of Australian defence policy to reconcile Australia's previous position on matters such as innocent passage, the exclusive economic zone and the archipelagic state with the principles in UNCLOS.

In 1991 I was appointed to set up the Maritime Studies Programme of the Royal Australian Navy (RAN) now the Sea Power Centre-Australia. This programme was established by the (then) Chief of Naval Staff in Australia, Vice Admiral M.W. Hudson AC RAN, with the objectives of bringing more intellectual rigour to the study of maritime strategy in the RAN, promoting awareness of maritime issues in the Navy and the wider Australian public, and promoting links between the RAN and other regional navies, as well as with strategic studies centres overseas concerned with maritime issues. On retiring from the RAN in 1993, I became the inaugural Director of the Centre for Maritime Policy at the University of Wollongong (now the Australian National Centre for Ocean Resources and Security or ANCORS), which was tasked with teaching, consulting and research on maritime affairs in Australia and the Asia-Pacific. From 2004 until 2018, I was associated with the Maritime Security Programme at the S. Rajaratnam School of International Studies (RSIS) at the Nanyang Technological University in Singapore, first as a Senior Research Fellow and later as an adviser to the programme.

My associations over the past 30 years have served to keep me abreast of regional maritime developments and provided extensive practical

x *Preface*

experience of strategic and political aspects of the law of the sea in the region. They have brought me into contact with some of the leading international figures in the broad areas of the law of the sea and international maritime affairs – people such as Mochtar Kusuma-atmadja, Etty Agoes and Hasjim Djalal (Indonesia); Tommy Koh and Robert Beckman (Singapore); B.A. Hamzah and Mak Joon Num (Malaysia); Kazumine Akimoto (Japan), Ed Miles, James Kraska and Mark Valencia (United States); Raphael Lotilla and Jay Batongbacal (Philippines); Phiphat Tangsubkul (Thailand); Dalchoong Kim and Jin-Hyun Paik (South Korea), Wu Shicun and Nong Hong (China), and Douglas Johnston, Edgar Gold and Elisabeth Mann-Borgese (Canada), some of whom are sadly no longer with us, as well as in Australia: Ivan Shearer, Martin Tsamenyi, Anthony Bergin, Don Rothwell, Clive Schofield, Stuart Kaye and Victor Prescott. I owe a considerable debt to these people and many others who have stimulated my interest in the issues covered in this book.

I also benefited greatly from my long-term experience as co-chair of the Maritime Cooperation Working Group established by the Council for Security Cooperation in the Asia Pacific (CSCAP) in 1994, and its various successor groups in CSCAP working on maritime issues.[1] In this respect, I am particularly grateful to the leading members of this Group over the years and take the liberty of mentioning R.M. Sunardi (Indonesia) (the other co-chair of the initial Maritime Security Working Group), Hideaki Kaneda, Toshiya Hoshino and Sumihiko Kawamura (Japan), Alberto Encomienda (Philippines), Gao Zhiguo and Xu Guangjiang (China), Stan Weeks and Ralph Cossa (United States), Peter Cozens, Joanna Mossop, Grant Hewison and Scott Davidson (New Zealand), Ian Townsend-Gault and Jim Boutilier (Canada), Premvir Das and Probal Ghosh (India), and Seo-Hang Lee (South Korea). Singularly and collectively, such people have enormous knowledge and experience of the law of the sea, maritime security and related issues in the Asia-Pacific, and working with them was an invaluable experience. Needless to say, our views on central issues did not always coincide.

In fact, I am indebted to all my fellow members of the CSCAP Maritime Cooperation Working Group for sharing with me their different perceptions of issues discussed in this book. They have alerted me to the realities that some key points are often lost in translation and what might seem settled and agreed in one forum, and by one country, is not necessarily so when seen through different eyes. A fascinating aspect was the different perspectives of the law of the sea held by various regional countries. The *CSCAP Memorandum on The Practice of the Law of the Sea in the Asia Pacific* specifically addressed areas of difference with the law of the sea in the region with a view to facilitating understanding of the different positions held by countries.[2]

I recently co-chaired a working group of the ASEAN Regional Forum (ARF) Expert and Eminent Persons' (EEPs) Group that conducted a study of lessons learnt and best practice with regard to preventing and managing incidents at sea in the Asia-Pacific region. I have also recently completed a study of maritime and border security arrangements in Papua New Guinea (PNG) for the PNG Government. In March 2017, I co-organised a workshop conducted by RSIS in Singapore on ASEAN perspectives of the freedoms of navigation.

While different perspectives of the law of the sea have always been evident in the region, the positions of regional countries on key issues, especially freedoms of navigation, have hardened over the years, particularly over the last decade. In many ways 2009 was the watershed year. The claims to an outer continental shelves in the region made that year and the American pivot to Asia put in train a series of events, including China's reclamation and militarisation of the features it claims in the South China Sea and the arbitration case brought by the Philippines in the South China Sea. Washington's freedom of navigation operations (FONOPS) have only served to put the different perspectives in sharper relief. This has been associated with a process of claim and counter claim, 'I am right and you are wrong' – a process that is sometimes referred to as 'lawfare'.

In this book I have tried to represent fairly these different views but am very conscious that this risks being seen as the protagonist of one particular view or the other. That has not been my intention. Rather my basic concern is the good governance of regional oceans and seas and the development of a stable maritime security regime in the Asia-Pacific region. That fundamentally requires the reconciliation of the different views. It is my hope that this book might make some progress towards that goal.

Notes

1 The proceedings of the meetings of the CSCAP Maritime Cooperation Working Group and its successors have been published as:

> Sam Bateman and Stephen Bates (eds), *Calming the Waters: Initiatives for Asia Pacific Maritime Cooperation*, Canberra Papers on Strategy and Defence No. 114, Strategic and Defence Studies, Centre, Australian National University, Autumn 1996.
> Sam Bateman and Stephen Bates (eds), *The Seas Unite: Maritime Cooperation in the Asia Pacific Region*, Canberra Papers on Strategy and Defence No. 118, Strategic and Defence Studies Centre, Australian National University, Spring 1996.
> Sam Bateman and Stephen Bates (eds), *Regional Maritime Management & Security*, Canberra Papers on Strategy and Defence No. 124, Strategic and Defence Studies Centre, Australian National University, Canberra, 1998.
> Sam Bateman and Stephen Bates (eds), *Shipping and Regional Security*,

Canberra Papers on Strategy and Defence No. 129, Strategic and Defence Studies Centre, Australian National University, Canberra, 1999.

Sam Bateman (ed.), *Maritime Cooperation in the Asia-Pacific Region: Current Situation and Prospects*, Canberra Papers on Strategy and Defence No. 132, Strategic and Defence Studies Centre, Australian National University, Canberra, 1999.

Institute for International Relations (IIR), *Objectives and Principles of Good Oceans Governance: The Contribution to Regional Security*, Proceedings of the 6th Meeting of the CSCAP Maritime Cooperation Working Group 24–25 August 1999, published by the Institute for International Relations, Hanoi, 1999.

Peter Cozens and Joanna Mossop (eds), *Capacity Building for Maritime Security Cooperation in the Asia Pacific*, Wellington: Centre for Strategic Studies New Zealand, 2005.

2 This memorandum was published in December 2002 as CSCAP Memorandum No. 6. The following CSCAP memoranda were published during my term of office with the several CSCAP maritime groups:

- CSCAP Memorandum No. 4 – Guidelines for Regional Maritime Cooperation (December 1997)
- CSCAP Memorandum No. 5 – Cooperation for Law and Order at Sea (February 2001)
- CSCAP Memorandum No. 6 – The Practice of the Law of the Sea in the Asia Pacific (December 2002)
- CSCAP Memorandum No. 8 – The Weakest Link? Seaborne Trade and the Maritime Regime in the Asia Pacific (April 2004)
- CSCAP Memorandum No. 12 – Maritime Knowledge and Awareness: Basic Foundations of Maritime Security (December 2007)
- SCAP Memorandum No. 12 – Guidelines for Maritime Cooperation in Enclosed and Semi-Enclosed Seas and Similar Sea Areas of the Asia Pacific (July 2008)

These memoranda are available on the CSCAP website at: www.cscap.org/

Acknowledgements

I have already acknowledged a number of leading people who have contributed, albeit unknowingly, to ideas in this book but I also have some other special acknowledgments to make. These include friends and colleagues at the University of Wollongong. These include Professor Martin Tsamenyi, former Director of ANCORS, and other staff at ANCORS, particularly Stuart Kaye (now Director of ANCORS), Clive Schofield, Mary Ann Palma and Chris Rahman; Professor Ted Wolfers of the Department of History and Politics, who alerted me first to many of the subtle political implications of the law of the sea; and Professor John Morrison, BHP Professor of Environmental Science, who has been an enthusiastic supporter of an inter-disciplinary approach to maritime policy and management. Also, at the University of Wollongong, I must mention Myree Mitchell, administrative officer at ANCORS, who has helped me in many ways over the years.

I have benefited greatly from my experiences in Singapore where there is a stimulating environment for the study of regional maritime security and associated issues. I have enjoyed my contacts at RSIS, especially with Kwa Chong Guan, Geoffrey Till, Jane Chan, Ralf Emmers and Richard Bitzinger, and with Ian Storey at the Institute of Southeast Asian Studies (ISEAS).

I am most grateful to ANCORS for financial support with the figures in this book, and to my old friend, John Nelson, who proofread the volume. Last but by no means least, I have to thank my wife, Lois, who has had to put up with a lot over the years and has so often had to adjust her life to suit my pursuit of the issues covered in this work.

Sam Bateman
Mooloolaba
June 2019

Abbreviations

ADIZ	Air Defense Identification Zone
AIS	Automatic Identification System
ANCORS	Australian National Centre for Ocean Resources and Security
ARF	ASEAN Regional Forum
ASEAN	Association of Southeast Asian Nations
ASL	archipelagic sea lane
CBM	confidence-building measure
CLCS	Commission on the Limits of the Continental Shelf
CRS	US Congressional Research Service
CSCAP	Council for Security Cooperation in the Asia Pacific
CSIS	Center for Strategic and International Studies (United States)
CUES	Code for Unplanned Encounters at Sea
DWFN	distant water fishing nation
EEZ	exclusive economic zone
FON	Freedom of Navigation
FONOP	Freedom of Navigation Operation
G77	Group of 77 (of developing countries)
IDSS	Institute of Defence and Strategic Studies (Singapore)
IMO	International Maritime Organisation
INCSEA	Incident at Sea Agreement
ISEAS	Institute of Southeast Asian Studies (Singapore)
ITLOS	International Tribunal for the Law of the Sea
LNG	liquid national gas
LPG	liquid petroleum gas
MCBM	maritime confidence-building measure
MMCA	Military Maritime Consultative Agreement
MOU	memorandum of understanding
MSR	marine scientific research

NBR	National Bureau of Asian Research (United States)
OPRF	Ocean Policy Research Foundation (Japan)
RAN	Royal Australian Navy
RSIS	S. Rajaratnam School of International Studies (Singapore)
UN	United Nations
UNCLOS	1982 UN Convention on the Law of the Sea
UNCLOS III	Third United Nations Conference on the Law of the Sea (1973–1982)

1 Introduction

Introduction

This book examines vexed issues with freedoms of navigation in the Asia-Pacific region.[1] Freedoms of navigation and the law of the sea more generally have become important strategic issues in this region. They are political tools that countries use as 'sticks' to beat each other with. China is usually the recipient of such attacks with calls for it to adhere more closely to a 'rules-based' order at sea with accusations that it is threatening the freedoms of navigation of other nations. Political use of the law of the sea, or what might be termed 'lawfare', is also evident in the sovereignty disputes in the region with arguments between the supporters of each side of the dispute claiming the law is on their side.

Politics provide the basic rationale for state action. Developments with the law of the sea over the years have shown a persistent interaction between law and politics. This is clearly the present situation in the Asia-Pacific region. While the interests of countries in the sea can coincide, they often also conflict. Maritime powers have a vested interest in the freedoms of navigation through archipelagos and international straits and elsewhere in regional seas, but many regional countries believe that unrestricted freedoms of navigation compromise their national security and threaten their marine environment. While the law of the sea sets the framework for resolving disputes, and potentially provides a dispute settlement mechanism, the solution to resolving these conflicts of interest will likely be a political one. This has been evident in the way in which under the influence of politics, the arbitral ruling in the case brought by the Philippines against China in the South China Sea has not had the impact that may have been anticipated.[2]

Historically, the politics of the law of the sea involved a clash of interests between coastal states and maritime *user* states, but the situation is now more complex. It is no longer sufficient to think simply of coastal state interests because coastal states might also be straits states,[3] archipelagic states, geographically disadvantaged states,[4] leading shipping or fishing countries, industrialised or developing countries, and so on with very different priorities in the law of the sea. For example, Singapore is both a straits state and a major maritime *user* state with mostly different interests in freedoms of navigation to those of its large neighbours, Indonesia and Malaysia.

This book explores the intersection of politics and the law with freedoms of navigation in the Asia-Pacific region. It draws heavily on concepts of international law, but of themselves, these are an excessively rigid framework in which to view freedoms of navigation in the region. Account should also be taken of powerful cultural, social and political values, as well as fundamental economic and strategic factors that influence law of the sea interests in the region. Some regional countries, notably Indonesia with its concept of *wawasan nusantara* (the 'archipelagic outlook'),[5] have a professed cultural affinity with the sea that leads them to seek maximum control over their adjacent waters.

A major 'stumbling block' to a broader common understanding of freedoms of navigation, and the law of the sea more generally, lies in domestic politics. Nationalism has become a major factor that prevents constructive negotiations to resolve differences of opinion and disputes in the region. It underpins the desire of many regional countries to place restrictions on the movements of foreign naval vessels in their adjacent waters.

Developments in the law of the sea affect political attitudes, strategic perceptions and regional relations throughout the Asia-Pacific, but particularly so in the narrow seas of East Asia. In turn, developments and political attitudes in the region have influenced the evolution of the law of the sea more generally. This is likely to be even more so in the future with the growing economic, political and maritime influence of the region. Considerations from the Asia-Pacific, East Asia in particular, will likely play a major role in the future development of ocean law at the global level.

In many ways, the outstanding problems of the freedoms of navigation and the law of the sea more generally now facing the international community are focused in the East Asian seas. These are perhaps the most disputed areas of maritime space in the world.[6] The perspectives of the law of the sea held by regional countries reflect political, economic, cultural and strategic considerations that are very different to those of the major Western powers that have dominated the law of the sea in the past. Interpretations of the relevant law can vary between countries, and these differences can constitute a potentially destabilising factor in regional relations and maritime security. They are evident when China and some other countries are accused of threatening the rules-based order of the seas that has applied for many years.[7] These countries may become increasingly assertive in pursuing their views against the traditional precepts of the rules-based order that have prevailed for many years.

Setting the scene

The maritime environment dominates the strategic geography of the Asia-Pacific region.[8] The sea and maritime issues are a major part of international relations in the region both between regional countries and between these countries and the rest of the world. Regional countries, historically more concerned about terrestrial issues and internal security, have become more strongly nationalistic about their offshore sovereignty and maritime security.

The significance of the sea to East Asian nations, in particular, is reflected in the size of their merchant shipping fleets, their dependence on seaborne trade and seafood, the emphasis on maritime capabilities in their defence forces, and the attention given to offshore sovereignty.

Most East Asian countries depend on the sea for foodstuffs, trade and longer-term economic prosperity and security, but there is growing concern over the depletion of fish stocks, the degradation of the marine environment and the destruction of habitats, such as seagrass beds, mangroves and coral reefs. With increased concern for energy security, many regional countries are investing heavily in offshore oil and gas exploration and exploitation.

Although the broader Asia-Pacific region is the overall strategic and political context for this book, the marginal seas of East Asia are its main focus. Northeast Asia and Southeast Asia are often regarded as separate strategic regions but, while their problems may be different, they are, in fact, closely entwined with each other. This is particularly so with maritime issues due to the linkages through seaborne trade, resource exploitation, the inherent mobility of naval forces, and the influence of China as a major maritime power in both sub-regions.

The countries of Northeast Asia face a major security issue with their dependence on the free movement of shipping through the confined waters of Southeast Asia. The phrase 'Malacca Dilemma' has been coined by China to refer to the potential for China to be greatly and adversely affected by blockages of key maritime trade routes, especially the Malacca Straits.[9] On the other hand, the straits states of Indonesia and Malaysia are aware of the potential strategic leverage than gain by their proximity to, and potential control over these strategic waterways.

This chapter provides the local knowledge of regional maritime issues that is an important basis for later chapters. It reviews significant issues

4   *Introduction*

with the contemporary regional maritime environment. These factors may be classified as either *enduring* features of the contemporary scene or as *dynamic* ones. Enduring features comprise the maritime geography of the region, especially features such as archipelagos, international straits, landlocked and geographically disadvantaged states, and enclosed and semi-enclosed seas. All these features figure prominently in the strategic geography of East Asia. Dynamic features include changes in regional relations, the rapid growth in regional seaborne trade, the growing scarcity of marine resources, increasing risks of marine pollution, the expansion of regional maritime forces (ships, submarines and aircraft), and changes in the regulatory regimes for maritime activities.

The maritime geography of East Asia is shown in Figure 1.1. It is very complex – perhaps the largest and most complicated area of maritime geography in the world. As a consequence of the extended maritime jurisdiction allowed by the 1982 UN Convention on the Law of the Sea (UNCLOS),[10] much of the maritime domain in this area is enclosed as the exclusive economic zones (EEZs) or archipelagic waters of coastal and archipelagic states. Some regional countries, notably Japan, Indonesia and the Philippines, which are mainly composed of islands, have very large areas of maritime jurisdiction. There are relatively few areas of high seas.

Table 1.1 shows the size of the maritime zones of East Asian countries (with maritime zones comprising EEZs, archipelagic waters and territorial sea), along with the ratio of maritime zones to land area. The latter ratio provides a crude indicator of a *maritime state* if this ratio is comfortably above 1:1. In absolute terms, Indonesia, Philippines, Japan and China have gained the largest maritime zones under UNCLOS although the ratio of maritime jurisdiction to land area for China is quite small being distorted by China's continental nature and very large land area.

The data in Table 1.1 also suggests the major 'winners' under UNCLOS in terms of additional maritime jurisdiction. The big 'winners' have clearly been the archipelagic and island states: Japan, Philippines, Indonesia and, to a lesser extent, Taiwan, with their large maritime/land ratios. Singapore is the exception here as, despite being an island state, it is at a significant geographical disadvantage as a result of being locked in by its two neighbours, Malaysia and Indonesia.

The 'losers' under UNCLOS in East Asia are the continental states with much of their coastline along gulfs or semi-enclosed seas. North Korea, Thailand and Cambodia are in this category. These are sometimes referred to as 'zone-locked' because they are locked in by the maritime zones of other countries. However, before assuming that these countries have relatively fewer maritime interests and concerns with the law of the sea, it is necessary to take a wider view of their maritime interests. For example,

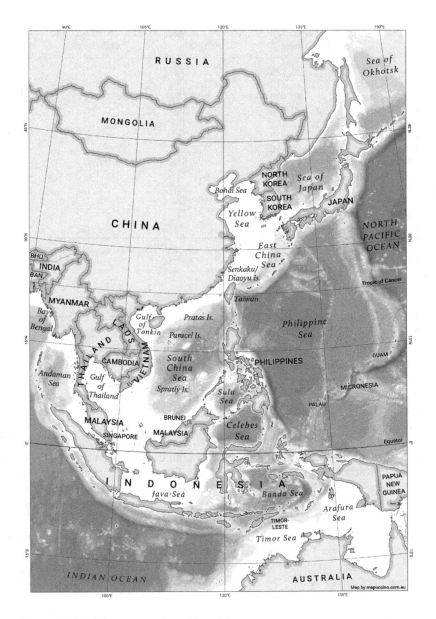

Figure 1.1 Maritime geography of East Asia.

Table 1.1 Maritime zones of East Asia

Country	Land area (sq km)	Maritime zones (sq km)	Maritime/land area ratio
Japan	370,370	3,861,000	10.4
North Korea	121,730	129,650	1.1
South Korea	98,400	348,478	3.5
China	9,600,000	1,355,800	0.1
Taiwan	32,360	392,381	12.1
Philippines	300,000	1,891,247	6.3
Vietnam	332,556	722,337	2.2
Thailand	414,001	324,812	0.6
Malaysia	332,649	475,727	1.4
Singapore	588	343	0.6
Indonesia	1,904,342	5,409,981	2.8
Brunei	5,765	24,352	4.2
Cambodia	181,041	55,564	0.3

Source: Based on H.J. Buchholz, *Law of the Sea Zones in the Pacific Ocean*, Singapore: Institute of Southeast Asian Studies, 1987, Table 6.

Thailand is an important distant water fishing nation (DWFN). This might help explain why Thailand did not ratify UNCLOS until 2011.

The coastline of continental East Asia stretches from the Sea of Okhotsk in the north to the Malay Peninsula in the south. Significant features of this coastline include the peninsulas, primarily the Kamchatka, Korean, Shandong and Malay Peninsulas, and the concave gulfs and bays, mainly the Yellow Sea, Bohai Sea, Gulf of Tonkin, and the Gulf of Thailand.

The other significant feature of the maritime geography of East Asia is the chain of off-lying archipelagos and islands, stretching from Sakhalin and the Kamchatka Peninsula through the Japanese archipelago and the Philippines archipelago to the Indonesian archipelago and northern Australia. The number of islands and groups of island lying between the continental coastline and the outer archipelagic chain, such as Taiwan and the Senkaku, Paracel and Spratly Islands, further complicates the situation. Achieving straight line maritime boundaries and clear sovereign jurisdiction over maritime areas and marine resources in such a region is an extremely difficult task.[11]

The archipelagic chain of East Asia is an effective barrier to ships and submarines moving between ports in mainland Asia and the wider Pacific Ocean. The Soviet Union perceived this vulnerability during the Cold War and developed strategies to deny US and allied forces access to its littoral areas, including 'bastions' for its ballistic missile submarines to operate with greater security within the enclosed seas of Northeast Asia.[12] Similarly, China's contemporary maritime strategy attaches importance to its 'outer perimeter' of defence provided by the archipelagic chain. Like the Russians, the Chinese are concerned about their surface and sub-surface forces being bottled up inside the archipelagic chain. Understandably, freedoms of navigation through the archipelagic chain are a strategic priority for China.

Special features

Archipelagos

The geographical definition of an archipelago is 'any large body of water with many islands' or 'the island groups in such a body of water'.[13] Then under UNCLOS Article 46, an 'archipelagic State' means 'a State constituted wholly by one or more archipelagos and may include other islands'. Under the law of the sea, there is a further distinction between *coastal* archipelagos (i.e. those adjacent to a coast) and *mid-ocean* archipelagos. The regime of the archipelagic state in UNCLOS Part IV may be applied to *mid-ocean* archipelagos subject to other criteria in UNCLOS Articles 46 and 47, relating to the integrity of the archipelago and the ratio of land to water, being met.

In the East Asian region, only the Philippine and Indonesian archipelagos meet the strict UNCLOS criteria for an archipelagic state and thus might be considered *legal* archipelagos. The Japanese and Taiwanese archipelagos, as well as Singapore, fail the criteria because they have too much land enclosed by any possible straight archipelagic baselines. Numerous smaller island groups fail the tests for an archipelagic state because they are either off-lying territories of countries that are not themselves comprised mainly of islands or groups of islands, or because with any conceivable set of baselines, they would exceed the allowable ratio of water to land. For example, the Mergui Archipelago off the southern coast of Myanmar, the Hoang Sa Archipelago in the Paracels, and the Trong Sa Archipelago in the Spratly Islands could not be classified as archipelagos under UNCLOS.

Enclosed or semi-enclosed seas

This geographical picture of concavity along the continental coastline of East Asia and the numerous off-lying archipelagos and islands create a chain of enclosed or semi-enclosed seas in East Asia subject to the regime of enclosed or semi-enclosed seas established by UNCLOS Part IX. From North to South, these seas are: Sea of Okhotsk, Sea of Japan, Yellow Sea, East China Sea, South China Sea, Gulf of Thailand, Java Sea, Sulu Sea, Celebes Sea, and Timor and Arafura Seas. The geography of some of these seas, such as the extremely concave Gulf of Thailand, is complex with two or more littoral states and overlapping claims to maritime jurisdiction. The situation is further complicated when the sea contains islands of varying sizes that are subject to sovereignty claims by more than one state.

The names of some of these seas have created a regional irritant with the Koreans resenting the name of the Sea of Japan for the body of water to the East of the Korean Peninsula and referring to it as the East Sea. In like vein, the Philippines now refers to the South China Sea as the West Philippine Sea while Vietnam refers to it as the East Sea. For people from outside the region, these issues may seem petty, but to the peoples of the countries involved, the names are a major expression of nationalism.

An *enclosed* or *semi-enclosed* sea is defined by UNCLOS Article 122 as:

> a gulf, basin or sea surrounded by two or more States and connected to another sea or the ocean by a narrow outlet or consisting entirely or primarily of the territorial seas and exclusive economic zones of two or more coastal States.

The second last 'or' in this definition is important. It provides for a geographical definition of an *enclosed* or *semi-enclosed* sea on the basis of its narrow physical connections with nearby bodies of water, as well as a legal definition that such a sea should consist entirely or primarily of the territorial seas and EEZs of two or more countries. This means that it does not have to be wholly surrounded or locked in by land. A gulf or a bay can also meet the criteria.

The regime established by UNCLOS Part IX is particularly important in East Asia. Under it, the bordering countries to the seas of East Asia have a binding obligation to cooperate with regard to managing marine living resources, protecting the marine environment and conducting marine scientific research.[14] Although the wording of this obligation is not as strong as it might be, it does recognise the fundamental importance of cooperation with these three activities to the effective management of enclosed and semi-enclosed seas.[15] The United States initially opposed the Part IX regime during negotiations on UNCLOS because it could provide an opening for the bordering states to introduce arrangements restricting other states from exercising high seas freedoms of navigation in these seas.[16] This explains the tendency of American officials to persist in referring to

Introduction   9

the South China Sea as 'international waters' when of course it is not – except for small 'do-nuts' of high seas, it comprises largely the EEZs of the bordering states.

International straits

A strait may be defined as 'a naturally-formed body of water linking two larger water bodies with one another'.[17] As will be discussed in Chapter 2, a special regime applies when a strait used for international navigation is wholly or partly contained within the territorial sea of one or more states. The maritime geography of East Asia with the off-lying island chain creates numerous straits, as well as other 'choke points' for shipping. These straits occur both along the coast of mainland Asia where the island chain presses close into the coast (e.g. the Tsushima Strait, the Taiwan Strait and the Straits of Malacca and Singapore), and through the off-lying islands (e.g. the Tsugaru Strait through the Japanese archipelago, the San Bernadino Strait in the Philippines, the Balabac Strait North of Borneo, and the Sunda and Lombok Straits through the Indonesian archipelago). Many of these straits are important for international shipping both for the ships making passage along the East coast of Asia between Southeast Asia and Northeast Asia, and for those heading into mainland Asian ports from the Americas and Oceania.

The Indonesian archipelago is a major barrier to sea movement between the Indian and Pacific Ocean. The various straits through and adjacent to this archipelago are of immense strategic importance. The straits through the archipelago between Singapore and Darwin in northern Australia now constitute the most significant shipping 'bottleneck' in the world. Vessels pass through this area carrying the sources of energy (oil, LNG and LPG) and raw materials essential for the maintenance of economic growth and survivability of China, Japan, South Korea and Taiwan, as well the large container ships on the main around the world route linking Europe to East Asia.

About 84,000 ships now pass through the Straits of Malacca and Singapore annually, about 23 per cent of which are the large tankers carrying the crude oil for the growing number of oil refineries in operation within East Asia, especially in China.[18] As a measure of the strategic importance of the Strait of Malacca, Robert Kaplan has referred to it as 'the Fulda Gap of the twenty-first-century multi-polar world'.[19]

This 'bottleneck' is most confined in the Malacca and Singapore Straits where, at its narrowest point in the Singapore Strait, the passage is a bare 2.5nm wide. These straits provide the most direct route through the 'bottleneck', but there is a least depth of about 25 metres and ships require an

10   *Introduction*

under keel clearance of 3.5 metres in accordance with the IMO's Rules for Vessels Navigating through the Straits of Malacca and Singapore issued by the International Maritime Organisation (IMO). Very large oil tankers over about 250,000 dwt may be outside these draught limitations. These ships may use Lombok and Makassar Straits further eastward although this might add about 1,000 nautical miles and three days' steaming to the passage. The Ombai–Wetar Straits around Timor are used by the large bulk carriers carrying iron ore from northwest Australia to northeast Asia.

An important consideration with the vulnerability of shipping is the possibility that littoral states may interpret the law of the sea in an overly nationalistic manner. Coastal states may threaten to disrupt the free flow of shipping, not only by posing a military threat to passing ships, but also by seeking to impose regulations on the freedoms of navigation on grounds of marine environmental protection or marine safety. Increased coastal state regulation of shipping passing through key international straits in the region is a particular concern of the major maritime user states. This was evident in 2006 when Australia introduced a compulsory pilotage regime in the Torres Strait despite the strong opposition of Singapore and the United States in particular.[20]

Sovereignty disputes

Numerous sovereignty disputes over features in the East Asian seas are another complicating factor of the strategic geography of the region. They fuel tensions at sea, prevent agreement on maritime boundaries, and hinder development of effective cooperation for managing regional seas and activities within them. The island disputes in the region include that over the Kurile (or Kuril) islands north of Japan (known in Japan as the Northern Territories) between Japan and Russia, and the one between Japan and South Korea over what Japan calls the Takeshima islands and Korea calls the Dokdo islands in the Sea of Japan (or East Sea), but the most complicating ones for the regional strategic environment are those in the East and South China seas.

The sovereignty dispute between China and Japan over the Senkaku islands (or Diaoyu islands for the Chinese) in the East China Sea involves two major powers tending to push their claims more strongly with regular incidents between their maritime security forces and fishing vessels. The islands are under the control of Japan but China argues that they have been part of Taiwan for many centuries, and thus are Chinese under the 'one China' policy. Just as with Taiwan's claims to features in the South China Sea, China does not dispute Taiwan's claim to the Diaoyu islands because to do so would admit to Taiwan's independent status.

Introduction   11

The United States is in a difficult position with the Senkaku/Diaoyu dispute. While it has repeatedly said that it takes no position on who has sovereignty over the islands, it has also acknowledged that the islands are covered by the 1960 United States–Japan Security Treaty because that treaty binds the United States to protect territories under the administration of Japan, and Japan has been administering the islands.[21] This in turn has led to a situation where China has become more assertive and resolute towards Japan in dealing the dispute because it considers that the apparent preparedness by Washington to accept that its security treaty with Japan extends to the islands is another indication of an anti-China alliance between the United States and Japan.

The situation in the South China Sea is the most notorious and problematic of all the jurisdictional problems in the East Asian seas.[22] This is due to several factors, particularly the number of countries involved in the disputes, the nationalistic sentiment engendered by the disputes and the strategic importance of the sea. Almost all the geographical features within the South China Sea are subject to sovereignty claims by several countries. China, Taiwan and Vietnam claim sovereignty over all the Spratly and Paracel islands while individual islands and reefs are claimed by Brunei, Malaysia and the Philippines. Nationalistic fervour is especially high in Vietnam, particularly in the context of its sovereignty disputes with China over the Paracels.

China's claims in the South China Sea have been subject to considerable speculation. This is largely due to differing interpretations of the dotted line that appears on some maps enclosing most of the South China Sea. This line is referred to in Chinese literature as the 'traditional maritime boundary line', 'the southernmost frontier', 'territorial limit', and so forth.[23] Western commentators talk about it as the 'U-shaped dotted line' or '9-dashed line'.[24] China first formally promulgated the line in 2009 in response to the joint submission in May 2009 by Malaysia and Vietnam to the Commission on the Limits of the Continental Shelf (CLCS) for an area of 'outer' or 'extended' continental shelf beyond their respective 200 nautical mile EEZs in the southern South China Sea.[25] Subsequently, Vietnam also made a separate submission in respect of parts of the northern central South China Sea. These submissions were provocative moves. Effectively they were one-sided claims to the resources of the seabed and subsoil in large parts of the South China Sea to the exclusion of the other claimants.

Initially it was thought that with the '9-dashed line', China was only saying that all the islands and reefs within the line are Chinese and that these generate maritime zones as allowed by international law. But recent articles by Chinese scholars claim that that as well as saying that the line reflects China's claim to the features that it encloses, the line also 'preserves China's historic rights in fishing, navigation, and other marine activities such as oil and gas development in the waters and on the continental shelf surrounded by the line',[26] It all depends on what is meant by 'historic rights'. Chinese scholars believe that the historic concept is still relevant in international law as the '9-dashed line' has a long history and pre-dates UNCLOS. However, Western scholars do not share this view believing that the concept of historic rights only applies to 'historic bays' as in UNCLOS Article 10(6).

The legal nature of the line was part of the ruling by the Arbitral Tribunal in The Hague established under Annex VII of UNCLOS on the dispute between China and the Philippines.[27] The tribunal ruled that China was not entitled to resource rights within the dashed line and strongly criticised China, and by implication, some other countries, for their reclamation activities contrary to their obligation to preserve and protect the marine environment. However, it did not declare this line illegal or invalid per se.[28] Hence it stands as acceptable geographical short-hand as defining the area within which China claims sovereignty over all features. The tribunal had no jurisdiction to rule on issues of sovereignty. The surprising feature of the ruling was the judgment that there are no 'fully entitled' islands in the Spratly Group entitled to an EEZ or continental shelf. This ruling was contrary to a substantial body of academic writings on the subject that considered, largely on the basis of state practice, that some features could be 'fully entitled' islands in the Spratlys rather than rocks and thus potentially entitled to a full set of maritime zones.[29]

China and the United States accuse each other of 'militarising' the South China Sea, but both are guilty in this respect. Much depends on what is meant by 'militarisation'.[30] China acknowledges that its reclaimed features have a military purpose, while the United States has raised the military 'ante' with its provocative FONOPS, increased naval deployments in the area, and its defence support for Southeast Asian claimants in the South China Sea. Beijing and Washington can both take some responsibility for the current situation in the South China Sea. They are sending conflicting signals to each other. China's plans to expand cooperative ties with countries along the Belt and Road Initiative (BRI) linking East Asia to the Middle East and Europe to promote trade and develop infrastructure are undermined by its aggressive posture in the South China Sea.

Along with these disputes over island features, the Taiwan situation is a dangerous aspect of the regional maritime scene. This has been identified as the most dangerous of the potential 'flash points' in the region largely because of the limited diplomatic avenues for addressing the dispute.[31] While time is on China's side, Beijing is resolutely committed to getting its way with Taiwan. President Trump's election and his generally erratic behaviour on Taiwan have been adding fuel to this already combustible situation. The regular passage of American warships through the Taiwan Strait while in accordance with international law have added to Washington's provocations of Beijing.[32]

None of these disputes, with the possible exception of Taiwan are likely to be resolved in the foreseeable future. Two primary factors – nationalism and access to marine resources – interact with each other to prevent their settlement. While international law provides guidance on the settlement of sovereignty disputes, fundamentally the process of dispute resolution is a political process requiring bilateral negotiation between the claimant parties. In the meantime while these sovereignty disputes exist, they are a complicating factor for good order at sea in the region.

Development of the freedoms of navigation

Freedoms of navigation are based on the framework provided by UNCLOS. This large and complex convention provides the constitution for the oceans and the basis for the types of jurisdiction that a country may exercise at sea in its various roles as a coastal, archipelagic, port or flag state. It sets out the rights and duties of a state with regard to the various uses of the oceans and prescribes the regime of maritime zones that establish the nature of state sovereignty and sovereign rights over ocean space and resources. UNCLOS also provides the principles and norms for navigational rights and freedoms, flag state responsibility, countering piracy, rights of visit, hot pursuit and regional cooperation, all of which are relevant to the maintenance of good order at sea. Other achievements of UNCLOS include the legal frameworks for preserving and protecting the marine environment, the sustainable development of marine living resources, marine scientific research, and dispute resolution.

UNCLOS now has a great many state parties,[33] but its effectiveness is still open to question in a number of areas.[34] Many examples can be found of apparent non-compliance with UNCLOS. These include the uses and abuses of territorial sea straight baselines, apparently illegal restrictions on the freedoms of navigation, and a reluctance to acknowledge the rights and duties of other states in the EEZ. It is a major limitation of UNCLOS as a foundation for a common understanding of freedoms of navigation in the region that the United States remains outside the Convention.

UNCLOS was formulated in a period when there was less concern for the health of the marine environment than there is at present. Norms and principles for preserving and protecting the marine environment have multiplied exponentially over the last 30 years or so. It is not surprising therefore that many of the apparent 'gaps' in UNCLOS arise in the area of environmental protection. The navigational regimes in UNCLOS provide an example of the underdeveloped level of concern for the marine environment evident in the 1970s. For example, the regimes of straits transit passage and archipelagic sea lanes (ASL) passage apply to 'all ships and aircraft',[35] and there is no direct right of the coastal or archipelagic state to prevent the passage of a vessel that could be a serious threat to the marine environment. Legal scholars have pursued this issue extensively over the years but so far there is not a satisfactory resolution of the issue. There is also the 'gap' in UNCLOS that there are several situations where no particular regime for jurisdiction over vessel-source pollution seems explicitly applicable, especially in geographical areas where a (non-suspendable) regime of innocent passage is applicable (e.g. under UNCLOS Article 45).[36]

The development of the law of the sea has been a continuing saga of tension between the interests of coastal states on the one hand and those of major maritime powers or user states on the other. Until the latter half of the twentieth century, the user states, who for the most part were major Western powers, clearly had the upper hand, including in maintaining maximum freedoms of navigation in global seas and straits. However, in the last 60 years or so, there has been a steady and pronounced trend towards more control by the coastal states over their littoral waters both geographically and jurisdictionally. This trend has been facilitated by the increased number of independent states as more countries around the world achieved their independence in the 1950s through to the 1970s. These countries with few exceptions have taken the coastal state view and sought wider control over their adjacent waters than had hitherto been acceptable under international law. These trends are evident in UNCLOS with agreement on the extension of the width of the territorial sea to 12 nautical miles and acceptance of the regimes of the EEZ and archipelagic state. These developments have all served to introduce more restrictions over freedoms of navigation than had existed previously.

The process of wider coastal state control is sometimes known as 'creeping sovereignty'. It occurs in a geographical sense with the extension of the territorial sea to 12 nautical miles and the introduction of the EEZ, archipelagic state and continental shelf regimes. Paradoxically, the United States started the process with the Truman Proclamation in 1945 proclaiming that the United States had the exclusive right to explore and exploit the mineral resources of its continental shelf beyond the (then) three-mile limit of the territorial sea. This was followed by other countries around the world, including some in South America that still adhere to a claim of a territorial sea out to 200 nautical miles. A common manifestation of 'creeping sovereignty' in East Asia is the use of territorial sea straight baselines, which have the impact of increasing the waters under the sovereignty of the coastal state than if normal baselines had been used.

The other form of wider coastal state control, known as 'creeping jurisdiction' or 'thickening jurisdiction', refers to either tightening regulations over activities over which the coastal state legitimately exercises jurisdiction, or extending regulations to activities which are usually regarded as not within a coastal state's jurisdiction. This trend was described by a leading American exponent of the law of the sea in the following terms,

> With the rare exception of outliers such as Singapore and Japan that prove the rule, many of the coastal states of Europe and much of the non-Western world are engaged in a relentless march to expand state control of the sea.[37]

Additional environmental controls over shipping and restrictions on marine scientific research are examples of the former type of extended jurisdiction while security zones and prohibitions on military activities in EEZs are examples of the latter. China, for example, is accused of 'thickening jurisdiction' when it asserts control over military surveillance in its EEZ and attempts to exercise fishing rights beyond its own EEZ.[38]

A naval concern of the United States is that these new maritime regulations on environmental grounds pose a threat to freedoms of navigation, a core American interest.[39] A meeting of American legal experts in 2006 agreed that management plans for marine protected areas, incorporating a variety of navigational restrictions, such as mandatory ship reporting, pilotage requirements and routeing measures, would increase in the future.[40]

The major development and conceptualising of the law of the sea during the 1960s and 1970s, reflected in UNCLOS, largely pre-date economic growth in East Asia. This economic growth has been associated to some extent with concurrent growth, actual and potential, in the political and strategic power and influence of the region. The power and influence of the region in regard to the development of the new law of the sea has followed a similar pattern. The so-called 'Asian Group' was rather ineffectual in negotiating UNCLOS at the Third United Nations Conference on the Law of the Sea (UNCLOS III), which took place between 1973 and 1982,[41] and with the notable exception of the archipelagic state regime, achieved little in terms of furthering regional interests in the law of the sea. A somewhat different convention may have resulted if it had been negotiated in the 1990s or the twenty-first century when Asian countries with their increased economic and political weight may have presented a more coordinated approach (for example, on some aspects of the UNCLOS navigational regimes), although achieving the necessary consensus would still have been difficult.

Although UNCLOS entered into force in November 1994, many of its provisions lack the clarity to remove all the uncertainties that exist at present, including some related to the freedoms of navigation. There are still many 'grey areas' with the law of the sea which require negotiation between interested parties. This is particularly so with provisions relating to the EEZ regime, which was new with UNCLOS. Problems arise because aspects of the regime, including those dealing with freedoms of navigation, are either uncertain or not universally accepted and because it requires countries to delimit new maritime boundaries with each other – in many instances where sovereign interests had not previously overlapped.[42]

Freedoms of navigation in East Asia

The maritime geography of East Asia means that freedoms of navigation are of great importance in the region both for the movement of merchant ships and naval vessels. Shipping is the main mode of transport for trade in the region. The free movement of commercial shipping through the seas of East Asia is vital to the economies of regional countries and unlawful restrictions on freedoms of navigation could have a serious impact on regional economies.

The United States, in particular, is concerned with its ability to conduct naval operations freely in the littoral seas of the region, as well as to deploy ships and submarines through regional straits, without restrictions imposed by coastal states other than those it regards as legitimate under international law. However, as will be discussed later in this book, all three of the navigational regimes established under UNCLOS (i.e. innocent passage, straits transit passage and archipelagic sea lanes passage), as well as the extension of high seas freedoms of navigation to EEZs, have issues with their implementation in the region. Some regional coastal states have introduced restrictions on freedoms of navigation, particularly military freedoms of navigation, that the United States and other extra-regional powers, regard as unlawful.

The importance of freedoms of navigation in regional waters is frequently mentioned in statements from forums in the region,[43] but there may be no common understanding of what freedoms of navigation are being referred to, or of the relevant law. Basic questions are evident. Are they freedoms for all vessels or just merchant ships? Or for warships? Does a particular freedom of navigation mean just sailing around in an area to assert a general freedom of navigation or does it mean challenging a specific jurisdictional claim made by another country? Is a particular freedom a freedom for all ships? Where does it apply? Should warships and fishing vessels also enjoy a particular freedom? What are valid restrictions on a particular freedom? Are military activities a freedom of navigation in an EEZ? These questions could go on and on. Unfortunately international law may not provide answers because the relevant law may be ambiguous, and international arbitration, particularly in cases related to military activities, is unlikely.[44] These questions are among those that later chapters in this book will address – without necessarily providing a clear answer.

The South China Sea has become the focus of the concern of extra-regional countries for freedoms of navigation in the seas of East Asia. China's widespread claims in the sea, its reclamation of features it claims, and the build-up of military facilities on these features, have led to widespread claims that it is threatening freedoms of navigation in the sea. Freedoms of navigation have relevance for both commercial and military vessels, but calls for a more aggressive regional response to China's activities are typically couched in terms of the alleged threat that Chinese actions pose to commercial shipping.[45] The verdict in the case brought by the Philippines against China on disputed matters in the South China Sea is often seen as lending support to these claims. Following the award, the Australian Government, for example, called on the Philippines and China to abide by the ruling as final and binding on both parties.[46] It went on to state that Australia will continue to exercise its international legal rights to freedom of navigation and overflight in the South China Sea, and to support the right of others to do so.[47]

While the United States is protesting a general threat by China to freedoms of navigation in the South China Sea,[48] at the heart of its protests are peculiarly American concerns that few regional countries share. In particular, these include the right to conduct hydrographic surveys and so-called 'military surveys' in the EEZs of another country without the permission of that country.[49] The United States argues that these activities, and military activities more generally, are an exercise of the high seas freedoms of navigation and overflight available in an EEZ.[50] Conversely, China argues that some of these activities do not have due regard to its rights in its EEZ, and that military surveys in particular are a form of either intelligence collection or marine scientific research.[51] These issues are discussed in detail in Chapter 3.

The United States and other extra-regional countries, including France and the United Kingdom, argue that because of China's assertive actions in the South China Sea, it poses a threat to freedoms of navigation in the sea, especially for the free movement of commercial shipping. However, China has repeatedly denied it poses such a threat. And with so much of

China's own trade passing through the sea, it is most unlikely that it would. Some countries, including the United States and Australia, are guilty of overstating the value of their trade in the South China Sea to justify their strategic involvement in the sea.[52]

In a press briefing in 2011, Admiral Bob Willard, the then Commander of the US Pacific Command, claimed that US$1.2 trillion of US trade crossed the South China Sea.[53] This was a marked overstatement. The United States' trade that most obviously crosses the South China Sea is that with ASEAN, but according to ASEAN trade statistics, America's trade with ASEAN in 2015 was just over US$212 billion.[54] It was unlikely to have been higher in 2011. Furthermore, a large proportion of that trade would have been carried by air, and much of that carried by sea would have been with the Philippines and Indonesia, two of ASEAN's biggest members, and may not have passed through the South China Sea. The figure quoted by Admiral Willard may have been for American trade with all of East Asia, including trade with China.

The South China Sea is undoubtedly the location of some of the world's busiest commercial shipping routes. According to a report from the Washington-based Center for Strategic and International Studies (CSIS), 30 per cent of global maritime trade passes through the South China Sea with a total value of approximately US$3.4 trillion.[55] In 2016, the value of China's trade transiting the South China Sea was $1.47 trillion, South Korea – $423 billion, Japan – $240 billion, Indonesia – $239 billion, and the US$208 billion. The South China Sea is a major trade route for crude oil.[56] In 2016, more than 30 per cent of global maritime crude oil trade passed through the South China Sea, of which 42 per cent was bound for China. About 90 per cent of the crude oil supplies for China, Japan and South Korea transited the sea.

Australian sources have also overstated Australia's trade crossing the South China Sea. With much of its seaborne trade passing through the confined archipelagic waters of Indonesia, Papua New Guinea and the Solomon Islands to its north, Australia has a strong interest in the freedoms of navigation.[57] However, Australia can also exaggerate its trade through the South China Sea to justify its strategic interest in the sea.[58] Its 2016 Defence White Paper says a lot about the South China Sea, both directly and indirectly. It noted that territorial disputes between claimants in the East China and South China Seas have created uncertainty and tension in Australia's region.[59] It said that Australia does not take sides on competing territorial claims in the South China Sea, but expressed concern about land reclamation and construction activities by claimants in the sea and about the possible use of artificial structures for military purpose.[60] It also makes much of the importance of a rules-based global order to Australia's security, with a clear message that some countries are not following these rules. But in making a big play of the South China Sea, the White Paper falls in line with what Greg Austin called 'The Pentagon's Big Lie about the South China Sea'.[61] For Austin, the lie is the claim that China's actions in the South China Sea threaten commercial shipping.

The Australian Defence White Paper replays Austin's sentiment. With regard to the free flow of trade through the South China Sea, it claimed that 'nearly two-thirds of Australia's exports pass through the South China Sea, including our major coal, iron ore and liquefied natural gas exports'.[62] However, this figure was an exaggeration.[63] The accurate figure, based on recent data for Australia's overseas trade,[64] is a little over 20 per cent and most of this is trade with China.[65] The White Paper actually disproves its own estimate with its map in its Figure 2 showing that most of Australia's sea freight to East Asia does not pass through the South China Sea.[66] Nor does the map show the busy trade route between eastern Australia, Japan and South Korea that passes to the east of the Philippines, rather than the South China Sea.

Australia's overseas trade crossing the South China Sea includes that with China (with a total of 23.9 per cent of two-way overseas trade), Thailand (2.8 per cent), Taiwan (1.9 per cent), Vietnam (1.4 per cent) and Hong Kong (1.2 per cent). And even these figures overstate Australia's dependence on the South China Sea, as it is only mainly trade with southern China that crosses the sea, and much trade is carried by air. These figures are based on overseas trade by value, which may hide the fact that a significant amount of trade by value is carried by air. In volume, maritime shipping is the main mode of transport for international trade, accounting for about 90 per cent of all the tonnage carried, but this is only about 73 per cent of the value of global trade.[67] Thus Australia's trade by volume across the South China Sea could provide a different result to that by value recognising the high volume of Australia's exports (coal, iron ore, LNG and other minerals) carried by sea, but it would still be nothing like 60 per cent.

Fundamentally different perspectives of the freedoms of navigation are evident in the Asia-Pacific region. Major powers, including ones from outside the region, argue the importance of freedoms of navigation in the sea mainly due to their concern for the free movement of commercial shipping across the sea, but in doing so, they can overstate the significance of their own maritime trade across the sea. Surprisingly, regional countries, with the exception of Japan, appear less concerned about freedoms of navigation for commercial shipping in regional seas, largely because of the extent of their trade with China. Regional countries are also less concerned about the rights of naval vessels to navigate freely in regional seas. They

20 *Introduction*

can also express concern that the assertion of rights to military freedoms of navigation in the region by extra-regional countries can be destabilising for the region, which after all is their own 'backyard'.

Outline

This book discusses how law, politics and strategy intersect to provide different perspectives of freedoms of navigation in the Asia-Pacific region. These freedoms are very important in this distinctively maritime region but also problematic with frequently little agreement as to what constitutes a particular freedom. Problems arise over interpreting the navigational regimes under the law of the sea, especially with regard to the rights of foreign warships to transit another country's territorial sea without prior notification or authorisation of the coastal state, and with determining the availability of high seas freedoms of navigation and overflight in an EEZ. The book explores these issues, referring in particular to the position of the main protagonists on these issues in Asian waters – the United States and China – with their strongly opposing views.

The following two chapters of this book address the main areas of difference with regard to freedoms of navigation in the region. Chapter 2 discusses the three main passage regimes in UNCLOS: innocent passage, transit passage through straits used for international navigation, and archipelagic sea lanes passage, and the issues with regard to their application in the Asia-Pacific region. Chapter 3 focusses on the EEZ regime, particularly the important area of disagreement related to the ability of a coastal state to introduce regulations that have the effect of denying high seas freedoms of navigation and overflight in all or part of its EEZ. Chapter 4 concludes the book with a discussion of the prospects for either resolving the different perspectives of the freedoms of navigation, or for developing confidence-building measures that would reduce the risks of maritime incidents.

Notes

1 This book will stick with the longstanding 'Asia-Pacific' term rather than the increasingly more popular 'Indo-Pacific', because the main focus of the book is the geo-strategic environment of East Asia and the Western Pacific.
2 The political factor is evident in most national responses to the arbitration case discussed in chapters in Fu-Kuo Liu and Jonathan Spangler (eds), *South China Sea Lawfare: Legal Perspectives and International Responses to the Philippines* v. *China Arbitration Case*, Taipei: Taiwan Center for Security Studies – South China Sea Think Tank, 2016, http://scstt.org/reports/2016/525/. The significance of the political factor was also evident in the statement that 'the

Introduction 21

current struggle in the South China Sea is primarily a political rather than a legal one', Ngo Di Lan, 'The Usefulness of "Redundant" Freedom of Navigation Operations', *AMTI Update*, 26 January 2018, https://amti.csis.org/usefulness-redundant-fonops/.
3 Straits states are those bordering a strait used for international navigation, such as the Malacca and Singapore straits.
4 A geographically disadvantaged state is one that did not gain much benefit in terms of the size of its area of maritime jurisdiction from the extension of jurisdiction introduced in UNCLOS, notably through the exclusive economic zone (EEZ), a new zone introduced by this convention, because they are locked in ('zone-locked') by other countries. Geographically disadvantaged states in the Asia-Pacific include North Korea, Singapore, Thailand and Cambodia.
5 For a discussion of Indonesia's approach to managing its archipelago, see chapters in Robert Cribb and Michele Ford (eds), *Indonesia beyond the water's edge: Managing an Archipelagic State*, Singapore: Institute of Southeast Asian Studies (ISEAS), 2009.
6 Clive Schofield, 'Maritime Cooperation in Contested Waters: Addressing Legal Challenges in East and Southeast Asian Waters' in Clive Schofield (ed.), 'Maritime Energy Resources in Asia – Legal Regimes and Cooperation', *NBR Special Report #37*, Seattle: The National Bureau of Asian Research, February 2012, p. 2.
7 Cavan Hogue, 'What rules based order?', *Pearls and Irritations*, 4 May 2018, https://johnmenadue.com/cavan-hogue-what-rules-based-order/.
8 This section draws on Sam Bateman, 'The East Asian Seas; Competing National Spheres of Influence' in Hance D. Smith, Juan Luis Suarez de Vivero and Tundi S. Agardy (eds), *Routledge Handbook of Ocean Resources and Management*, Abingdon: Routledge, 2015, pp. 524–538.
9 Marc Lanteigne, 'China's Maritime Security and the "Malacca Dilemma"', *Asian Security*, Vol. 1, No. 2, 2008, pp. 143–161.
10 United Nations Convention on the Law of the Sea, December 10, 1982, UN A/CONF.62/122, 1982, reprinted in *The Law of the Sea Official Text of the United Nations Convention on the Law of the Sea with Annexes and Index*, UN Sales No. E.83.V.5, 1983 and 21 I.L.M. 1261, 1982.
11 Sam Bateman, 'Sovereignty as an Obstacle to Effective Oceans Governance and Maritime Boundary Making – the Case of the South China Sea' in Clive Schofield, Seokwoo Lee and Moon-Sang Kwon (eds), *Limits of Maritime Jurisdiction*, Leiden: Brill Academic Publishers, 2013, pp. 201–224.
12 Christopher Cowan, 'Anti-access/Area Denial: Not as New as You Might Think', *The Strategist*, 13 September 2016, www.aspistrategist.org.au/anti-accessarea-denial-not-new-might-think/.
13 Definition from *The Macquarie Concise Dictionary*, 2nd edn, Macquarie University: The Macquarie Library, 1996, p. 43.
14 UNCLOS Article 123.
15 Ian Townsend-Gault, 'Maritime Cooperation in a Functional Perspective' in Schofield, 'Maritime Energy Resources in Asia', p. 11.
16 Mitja Grbec, *Extension of Coastal State Jurisdiction in Enclosed and Semienclosed Seas – A Mediterranean and Adriatic Perspective*, Abingdon: Routledge, 2014, p. 18.
17 L.M. Alexander 'Geographical Perspectives on International Navigation' in Jon Van Dyke, Lewis M. Alexander and Joseph R. Morgan (eds), *International*

22 *Introduction*

   Navigation: Rocks and Shoals Ahead? Honolulu: The Law of the Sea Institute, 1988, pp. 73–82.
18 Marcus Hand, 'Malacca and S'pore Straits Traffic Hits New High in 2016, VLCCs Fastest Growing Segment', *Seatrade Maritime News*, 13 February 2017, www.seatrade-maritime.com/news/asia/malacca-and-s-pore-strait-traffic-hits-new-high-in-2016-vlccs-fastest-growing-segment.html.
19 Robert Kaplan, *Monsoon – The Indian Ocean and the Future of American Power*, New York: Random House, 2010, p. 261.
20 Sam Bateman and Michael White, 'Compulsory Pilotage in the Torres Strait: Overcoming Unacceptable Risks to a Sensitive Marine Environment', *Ocean Development and International Law*, Vol. 40, No. 2, pp. 184–203.
21 Mark E. Manyin, 'Senkaku (Diaoyu/Diaoyutai) Uslands Dispute: US Treaty Obligations', *Congressional Research Service Report 7–5700*, 25 September 2012.
22 International Crisis Group, 'Stirring up the South China Sea (I)', *Asia Report No. 223*, Brussels: International Crisis Group, 23 April 2012.
23 Zhigou Gao, 'The South China Sea: From Conflict to Cooperation', *Ocean Development and International Law*, Vol. 25, 1994, p. 346.
24 A comprehensive analysis of this line with its history is available in US State Department, 'China's Maritime Claims in the South China Sea', *Limits in the Seas No. 143*, 5 December 2014.
25 Sam Bateman and Clive Schofield, 'Outer Shelf Claims in the South China Sea: New Dimension to Old Disputes', *RSIS Commentary 65/2009*, 1 July 2009.
26 Gao, Zhiguo and Jia, Bing Bing, 'The Nine-Dash Line in the South China Sea: History, Status, and Implications,' *The American Journal of International Law*, Vol. 107, No. 1, 2013, pp. 98–124.
27 Permanent Court of Arbitration (PCA), The South China Sea Arbitration (The Republic of the Philippines V. the People's Republic of China, *Press Release*, The Hague, 12 July 2016, https://pca-cpa.org/wp-content/uploads/sites/175/2016/07/PH-CN-20160712-Press-Release-No-11-English.pdf.
28 Robert Beckman 'Game Changer in the Maritime Disputes', *RSIS Commentary 180/2016*, 18 July 2016, www.rsis.edu.sg/wp-content/uploads/2016/07/CO16180.pdf.
29 Sam Bateman, 'Obama at Midway: Picking and Choosing the Law of the Sea', *The Interpreter*, 2 September 2016, www.lowyinterpreter.org/post/2016/09/02/Obama-at-Midway-Picking-and-choosing-the-law-of-the-sea.aspx.
30 Mark J. Valencia, 'Who Is Militarizing the South China Sea?' *The Diplomat*, 20 December 2015, http://thediplomat.com/2015/12/who-is-militarizing-the-south-china-sea/.
31 Brendan Taylor, *The Four Flash Points – How Asia goes to War*, Carlton, Vic.: La Trobe University Press, 2018.
32 Ralph Jennings, 'US Navy Frequents Taiwan Strait to Send China Message', *VOA News*, 1 March 2019, www.voanews.com/a/us-navy-frequents-taiwan-strait-to-send-china-message/4809103.html.
33 Cambodia, North Korea and the United States are the regional countries that are not parties to UNCLOS.
34 Sam Bateman, 'UNCLOS and Its Limitations as the Foundation for a Regional Maritime Security Regime', *Korean Journal of Defense Analysis*, Vol. 19, No. 3, Fall 2007, pp. 27–56.
35 UNCLOS Articles 38(1) and 53(2).

36 Erik Jaap Molenaar, 'Navigational Rights and Freedoms: Grey Areas and Scope for Regional Agreement' in Sam Bateman (ed.), *Maritime Cooperation in the Asia-Pacific Region: Current Situation and Prospects*, Canberra Papers on Strategy and Defence No. 132, Strategic and Defence Studies Centre, Australian National University, Canberra, 1999, pp. 98–108.
37 James Kraska, *Maritime Power and the Law of the Sea*, New York: Oxford University Press, 2011, p. 13.
38 Caitlyn L. Antrim and George Galdorisi, 'Creeping Jurisdiction Must Stop', *US Naval Institute Proceedings*, Vol. 137, No. 4, April 2011, pp. 65–71.
39 James Kraska, 'Missing the Boat', *Armed Forces Journal*, April 2009, www.armedforcesjournal.com/missing-the-boat/.
40 Craig H. Allen, 'Moderator's Report – Legal Experts Workshop on the Future Global Legal Order', *Naval War College Review*, Vol. 60, No. 4, 2007, p. 83.
41 Edward L. Miles, *Global Ocean Politics – The Decision Process at the Third United Nations Conference on the Law of the Sea 1973–1982*, The Hague: Martinus Nijhoff Publishers, 1998, p. 24.
42 Prior to UNCLOS, maritime boundaries were only required if countries were adjacent to each other, had territory lying within six nm of each other, or had overlapping continental shelves. Now with the EEZ regime, countries require maritime boundaries if they have territory within 400 nm of each other (even 700 nm in certain circumstances of the continental shelf), and the location of a boundary can have a large effect on the size of a country's maritime jurisdiction.
43 For example, the Chairman's Statement from the 25th ASEAN Regional Forum held in Singapore, 4 August 2018, noted in its paragraph 7 that 'The Ministers reaffirmed the importance of maintaining and promoting peace, security, stability, safety and freedom of navigation in and overflight above the South China Sea'. http://aseanregionalforum.asean.org/files/library/ARF%20Chairman's%20Statements%20and%20Reports/The%20Twentyfifth%20ASEAN%20Regional%20Forum/Final_Chairmans_Statement_of_the_25th_ARF.pdf.
44 In the case of disputes concerning military activities, UNCLOS Article 298 allows states to opt out of compulsory procedures entailing binding decisions.
45 James Laurenceson, 'Economics and Freedom of Navigation in East Asia', *Australian Journal of International Affairs*, 2017, http://dx.doi.org/10.1080/10357718.2017.1301374, p. 2.
46 The Hon Julie Bishop MP, 'Australia supports peaceful dispute resolution in the South China Sea', Media release, 12 July 2016, https://foreignminister.gov.au/releases/Pages/2016/jb_mr_160712a.aspx.
47 Ibid.
48 Sam Bateman, 'What is the US Protesting in the South China Sea?' *East Asia Forum*, 20 October 2015, www.eastasiaforum.org/2015/10/20/what-is-the-us-protesting-in-the-south-china-sea/.
49 James Kraska, *Maritime Power and the Law of the Sea*, New York: Oxford University Press, 2011, p. 275.
50 Raul (Pete) Pedrozo, 'Preserving Navigational Rights and Freedoms: The Right to Conduct Military Activities in China's Exclusive Economic Zone', *Chinese Journal of International Law*, Vol. 9, No. 1, March 2010, pp. 9–30.
51 Zhang Haiwen, 'Is It Safeguarding the Freedom of Navigation or Maritime Hegemony of the United States?—Comments on Raul (Pete) Pedrozo's Article on Military Activities in the EEZ', *Chinese Journal of International Law*, Vol. 9, No. 1, March 2010, pp. 31–48.

Introduction

52 Laurenceson, 'Economics and Freedom of Navigation in East Asia'.
53 White House, Office of the Press Secretary, 'Press Briefing by NSA for Strategic Communications', Ben Rhodes and Admiral Robert Willard, 'US Pacific Command', Moana Surfrider Hotel, Honolulu, Hawaii, 13 November 2011, https://obamawhitehouse.archives.gov/the-press-office/2011/11/13/press-briefing-nsa-strategic-communications-ben-rhodes-and-admiral-rober.
54 ASEAN External Trade Statistics Table 20 – Top Ten ASEAN Trade Partner Countries/Regions, 2015, https://asean.org/wp-content/uploads/2016/11/Table20_as-of-6-dec-2016.pdf.
55 Linda B. Paul, 'The Need for Open Sea Lines of Communication in the South China Sea', *PacNet #59*, 21 August 2018, www.csis.org/analysis/pacnet-59-need-open-sea-lines-communication-south-china-sea. AJOT, 'More than 30% of Global Maritime Crude Oil Trade Moves through the South China Sea', *American Journal of Transportation*, 27 August 2018, www.ajot.com/news/more-than-30-of-global-maritime-crude-oil-trade-moves-through-the-south-china-sea.
56 AJOT, 'More than 30% of global maritime crude oil trade moves through the South China Sea', *American Journal of Transportation*, 27 August 2018, https://www.ajot.com/news/more-than-30-of-global-maritime-crude-oil-trade-moves-through-the-south-china-sea.
57 Sam Bateman, 'Some Thoughts on Australia and the Freedoms of Navigation, *Security Challenges*, Vol. 11, No. 2, 2015, pp. 57–66.
58 Sam Bateman, 'Australia's Flawed Position on the South China Sea', *East Asia Forum*, 10 March 2016, www.eastasiaforum.org/2016/03/10/australias-flawed-position-on-the-south-china-sea/#more-49860.
59 Australian Government, *Defence White Paper 2016* (Canberra: Department of Defence, 2016), paragraph 1.6.
60 *Defence White Paper 2016*, paragraph 2.77.
61 Greg Austin, 'Mountains out of Molehills: The Pentagon's Big Lie about the South China Sea', *The Diplomat*, 24 February, 2016, https://thediplomat.com/2016/02/mountains-out-of-molehills-the-pentagons-big-lie-about-the-south-china-sea/.
62 *Defence White Paper 2016*, paragraph 2.72.
63 Sam Bateman, 'What Are Australia's Interests in the South China Sea?', *The Strategist*, 28 May 2015, www.aspistrategist.org.au/what-are-australias-interests-in-the-south-china-sea/.
64 Department of Foreign Affairs and Trade, Composition of Trade Australia 2013–14, Table 7, http://dfat.gov.au/about-us/publications/Documents/cot-fy-2013-14.pdf.
65 Bateman, 'Australia's Flawed Position on the South China Sea'.
66 *Defence White Paper 2016*, Figure 2, p. 70.
67 Modal shares of world trade by volume in 2008 were 89.8 per cent by sea, 10.0 per cent overland, and 0.3 per cent by air. By value the shares were very different – 72.7 per cent by sea, 14.3 per cent overland, and 13.0 per cent by air. Modal Shares of World Trade by Volume and Value, 2008, *The Geography of Transport Systems*, https://transportgeography.org/?page_id=3950.

2 Navigational regimes

Innocent passage

The right of innocent passage is well-rooted in state practice. However, the right has been progressively more narrowly defined over the years as is evident in the list of activities contrary to innocent passage set out in UNCLOS Article 19(2). This provides more detailed limitations on innocent passage than was provided in the equivalent article in the 1958 Geneva Convention on Territorial Sea and the Contiguous Zone.[1]

The rules applicable to innocent passage are contained in Part II Section 3 of UNCLOS. It is the most restrictive of the passage regimes in UNCLOS. It may be suspended in certain circumstances,[2] submarines must travel on the surface and show their flag,[3] and ships are prevented *inter alia* from operating organic aircraft,[4] or carrying out of research or survey activities.[5] It is a 'right' and not a 'freedom'. It applies only to ships and there is no associated right of overflight. During the development of UNCLOS it became apparent that additional regimes would be required beyond innocent passage. These were necessary to accommodate the interests of maritime user states in the light of acceptance of the concepts of the archipelagic state and the EEZ, and the extension of the maximum width of the territorial sea from three to 12 nautical miles.[6] The maritime user states wanted a more liberal regime than innocent passage through archipelagic waters and straits used for international navigation.

Two aspects of the innocent passage regime are problematic in East Asia. The first is the issue of the innocent passage of warships through the territorial seas of regional countries. Many countries regard the obligation to allow foreign warships the right of innocent passage through their territorial sea as a significant limitation on their sovereignty and a potential threat to their national security. The second issue is the requirement that where the high seas or territorial sea are converted into internal waters by straight baselines, the right of innocent passage be preserved in those waters.[7] It is a problem because so many regional countries have claimed straight baseline systems purporting to claim additional areas of internal waters. While a strict reading of UNCLOS Article 8(2) indicates that a right of innocent passage should still exist in these waters, generally the countries concerned have not conceded this in their national legislation.

On the first issue, there are about 47 countries around the world that have some form of a requirement for prior notification or authorisation of warship entry into the territorial sea.[8] This reflects the division of view between, on the one hand, major naval powers wishing to secure their naval mobility, and on the other, the coastal states that regard the unannounced passage of foreign warships through their territorial sea as a threat to their security.[9] The states with the requirement include the following East Asian countries: Cambodia, China, South Korea, North Korea, Indonesia, Philippines and Vietnam.[10] China specifically stipulated the requirement in a Declaration on ratifying UNCLOS that included the following statement:

> The People's Republic of China reaffirms that the provisions of the United Nations Convention on the Law of the Sea concerning innocent passage through the territorial sea shall not prejudice the right of a coastal state to request, in accordance with its laws and regulations, a foreign state to obtain advance approval from or give prior notification to the coastal state for the passage of its warships through the territorial sea of the coastal state.[11]

The arguments against prior authorisation or notification are supported by the fact that while negotiating UNCLOS, several countries sought to have the requirement contained in the Convention but were unsuccessful in achieving a consensus on this issue.[12] Ambassador Tommy Koh of Singapore, the Conference President at the time, went on record saying:

> I think the Convention is quite clear on this point. Warships do, like other ships, have a right of innocent passage through the territorial sea, and there is no need for warships to acquire the prior consent or even notification of the coastal State.[13]

In the closing stages of the Cold War, the United States and the Soviet Union reached a uniform interpretation of the innocent passage regime that stated: 'All ships, including warships, regardless of cargo, armament or means of propulsion, enjoy the right of innocent passage through the territorial sea in accordance with international law, for which neither prior notification nor authorization is required.'[14] This reflected a change in the

Soviet Union's previous position of requiring prior notification of warship transit. While the interpretation applies only to the United States and the Soviet Union, it does lend general support to the view that prior notification or authorisation is not a requirement.

A similar agreement between the United States and China might establish an important precedent for the region that would remove one of the 'wicked problems' of maritime security.[15] This would depend on China changing its mindset from that of a continental power to that of a true maritime power. Major maritime powers have typically sought maximum freedoms of navigation with greater advantages to be obtained from not giving prior notification of transits by their warships through the territorial sea of another state while allowing foreign warships to transit in their own territorial sea without notification. However, China's mindset in this regard might be so entrenched as to make this unlikely.

A coastal state may establish restrictions upon the exercise of innocent passage of foreign vessels for reasons such as traffic management, resource conservation and environmental protection,[16] but these should not effectively deny the right of innocent passage.[17] In certain circumstances, a coastal state may suspend innocent passage temporarily in specified areas of its territorial sea but these arrangements should be non-discriminatory in their effect as between different classes of ship and different countries.[18] Rothwell perceived that this issue of discrimination was a factor when he concluded that the Indonesian restrictions on the Portuguese protest vessel entering Indonesian territorial waters in March 1992 were improper.[19]

The determination of whether or not the passage of a particular vessel is non-innocent might be difficult. The burden of proving non-innocent passage appears to rest with the coastal state as the enforcement authority.[20] This might be problematic in terms of proving whether a vessel is engaging in one of the activities in UNCLOS Article 19(2) that are deemed to be 'prejudicial to the peace, good or security of the coastal State'. For example, it would be hard to prove an act 'aimed at collecting information to the prejudice of the defence or security of the coastal State'.[21] There might be no external indication, such as additional aerials to collect communications or electronic intelligence, that such an act was being carried out.

A particular issues arises if the warship is conducting the passage purely for exercising the right of innocent passage without prior notification or authorisation as required by the coastal state. This might be evident to the coastal state by virtue of an obvious diversion from the direct navigational route. The coastal state could well argue then that the diversion was not part of 'continuous and expeditious' passage as required by UNCLOS Article 18(2), and also, that the purpose of the diversion in itself suggested an activity 'prejudicial to the peace, good order or security of the coastal State' contrary to the meaning of innocent passage in UNCLOS Article 19(1). In this regard, the diversion might fall within the 'catch-all' phrase of 'any other activity not having a direct bearing on passage' in UNCLOS Article 19(2)(l). These considerations might apply to the freedom of navigation operations (FONOPS) conducted by the United States and other powers past islands in the Spratly Group in the South China Sea that are remote from any normal shipping route.

In his detailed analysis of the innocent passage regime, which admittedly is biased towards the interests of coastal states, Ngantcha reaches a conclusion that 'the weight of opinion is that warships do not have an independent right of passage in the territorial sea but a conditional one' that is subject to coastal state control.[22] An American naval lawyer writing in 1984 acknowledged the existence of a large number of states requiring prior notification or authorisation and judged that there were 'uncharted waters' ahead with the non-innocent passage of warships.[23] However, the position of the United States on this issue remains firm and, if anything, may even have hardened further over later decades.

A requirement for prior notification is different to that for prior authorisation. It is rather less objectionable than the one for prior authorisation and could even fall within the scope of UNCLOS Article 21(1)(a), which allows coastal states to adopt laws and regulations in respect of the safety of navigation and the regulation of maritime traffic.[24] Apart from the legal aspect, the arguments for prior notification, but not prior authorisation, are not without merit in a political context. Scovazzi has argued in the context of prior notification of passage through an international strait, but his point is also relevant to innocent passage, 'a mere notification only makes the bordering state aware of what will happen' and 'It is hard to reconcile secrets with the general obligation to cooperate, which is the basis of international environmental law'.[25] It could equally well be argued that secrecy of movement is also incompatible with the processes of maritime confidence and security building and transparency that should lead to a more peaceful region.

In view of the many states leaning towards a requirement for prior notification or authorisation, Churchill and Lowe have observed that 'there seems to be a general sense that the question is, for all practical purposes, best left without a clear answer'.[26] At this stage there might appear to be no customary rule one way or the other for the innocent passage of warships through the territorial sea.[27] The arguments in support of at least, prior notification of warship transit through a territorial sea may well gather strength in the East Asia, given the number of regional countries that require prior notification or authorisation of warship transit. It will come down to an argument between on the one hand, a majority of regional coastal and archipelagic states, and on the other, the United States exercising 'the incredible behaviour congenial to a major sea power',[28] supported possibly by Russia and Japan, as well as some extra-regional Western countries such as the United Kingdom, Australia and France. Deciding factors may well be consideration of idealistic principles, such as friendliness, cooperation, trust, transparency and good neighbourly behaviour.

There is also some evidence of a practice that where a state has some requirement for prior notification of warships transit, this might be met on an informal basis by a low-level contact or briefing note by a naval attaché to the local naval authorities.[29] The author is aware that this practice has been followed in past years by both the United States and Australia in advance of the transit of their warships though the Indonesian archipelago. This practice constitutes an important confidence-building measure that reduces the risk of disputation, or even conflict, over the issue.[30]

The second issue with innocent passage in the region, which is the widespread use of straight baselines in the region, can be dealt with relatively briefly.[31] UNCLOS Article 5 provides for normal territorial baselines basically tracking along the low-water line along the coast. However, in particular restricted geographical circumstances, straight baselines may be employed. UNCLOS Article 7 establishes three main criteria for drawing these baselines. First, and crucially, they should only be used in localities 'where the coastline is deeply indented, or if there is a fringe of islands along the coast in its immediate vicinity.' Second:

> [t]he drawing of straight baselines must not depart to any appreciable extent from the general direction of the coast, and the sea areas lying within the lines must be sufficiently linked to the land domain to be subject to the regime of internal waters.

Third, account may be taken of economic interests peculiar to the region concerned, the reality and the importance of which are clearly evidenced by long usage. These seemingly strict criteria have been interpreted very flexibly, or even ignored in practice, by countries in East Asia.

Many regional countries (i.e. Cambodia, China, Japan, North Korea, South Korea, Malaysia, Myanmar, Russian Federation, Thailand and Vietnam) have used straight baselines for parts of their coasts which are neither deeply indented or with a 'fringe' of islands. For example, in 1996, China claimed a system of straight baselines along most of its mainland coast and around the Paracel islands in the South China Sea.[32] In another extreme example, Malaysia has employed a system of implicit straight baselines by proclaiming outer limits of the territorial sea, which because they are straight, are therefore implicitly based on straight lines.[33] In most cases, the use of straight baselines has been controversial and judged by the United States, in particular, to be 'excessive', and thus subject to diplomatic protest, as well as the operational assertion of navigational rights by American ships under the Freedom of Navigation (FON) program.[34]

The main reason for countries using straight baselines is that it increases their claimed area of maritime jurisdiction. The operational implication of straight baselines is that it increases the area where the coastal state might seek to restrict the freedoms of navigation and overflight available to other countries.

Vietnam, for example, has proclaimed a 'radical' straight baseline system.[35] As shown in Figure 2.1,[36] this system uses nine turning points five of which are more than 50 nm offshore. This is hardly within the requirements of a straight baseline mainly because the coastline in the area is not 'deeply indented and cut into'.[37] Vietnam is thus claiming a large area of internal waters inside these baselines where according to the Law of the Sea of Vietnam, as updated in 2012, foreign warships may only enter 'at the invitation of the Vietnamese Government or in accordance with the agreement between the competent authorities of Viet Nam and the flag States',[38] or in other words, with the prior authorisation of Vietnam. Similarly according to this law, foreign warships are required to give prior notification of entering the territorial sea of Vietnam.[39] Despite these requirements in law, Vietnam has not taken practical steps to enforce these requirements and has appeared relaxed about US FONOPS to protest the requirements.[40]

Transit passage

The regime of transit passage gives all ships and aircraft the right to travel through straits used for international navigation in their normal operational mode on, under or over the sea.[41] Recognition of a 12 nautical mile limit to the territorial sea of a coastal state in UNCLOS had a considerable impact upon navigation through international straits. It has been estimated that there were over 100 straits around the world with least breadths of between six and 24 nautical miles that had previously included high seas 'corridors', but became enclosed within the territorial sea of one or more coastal states with acceptance of the 12 nautical mile limit.[42]

Without this regime, only the more restrictive innocent passage regime would have been available through these straits. The principles governing transit passage are set out in Section 2 of Part III of UNCLOS. Such passage is defined as the exercise of the freedom of navigation and overflight by

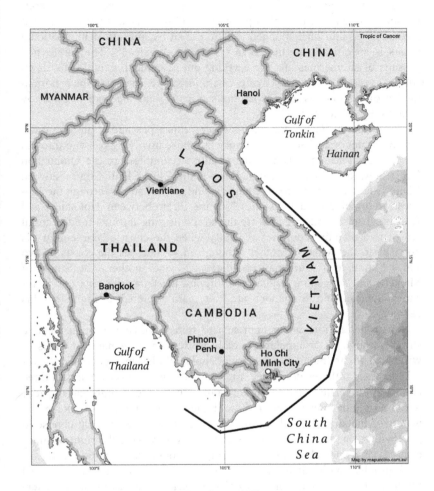

Figure 2.1 Territorial sea straight baselines of Vietnam.

ships and aircraft through an international strait 'between one part of the high seas or an exclusive economic zone and another part of the high seas or exclusive economic zone'.[43] Passage must be 'continuous and expeditious', but this does not preclude entering or leaving a state bordering the strait, subject to the entry requirements of that state.[44]

The right of straits' transit passage has particular significance for naval and air deployments. It is the view of the United States and other major naval powers, that under this regime, 'Submarines may pass through straits submerged, naval task forces may conduct formation steaming, aircraft carriers may engage in flight operations, and military aircraft may transit unannounced and unchallenged'.[45] The transit by aircraft of international straits is specifically permitted in UNCLOS Article 38. The submerged passage of submarines and the carrying out of tactical activities by naval surface vessels, including flying operations, are seen as 'their normal modes of continuous and expeditious transit', and thus are allowed by UNCLOS Article 39(1)(c).

The straits in East Asian waters where transit passage might apply fall into two categories. The first category are those involving passage through the territorial sea of only the one country. Examples are the Qiongzhou Strait between Hainan and mainland China, the Cheju Strait between Cheju Island and the Korean peninsula, and several straits through the Japanese archipelago, such as the Tsugaru Strait between Hokkaido and Honshu. The second category are the straits passing through the territorial sea of two or more countries typically when the coast of one country is opposite to the coast of another although in some cases the coasts of two states littoral to a strait may be adjacent to one another. The Straits of Malacca and Singapore which pass through the territorial seas of Malaysia, Indonesia and Singapore are the main regional example of this category.

Japan has an interesting approach to transit passage through the five straits through its archipelago, which are less than 24 nautical miles in width and where transit passage might apply. While Japan generally claims a 12 nautical mile territorial sea, for security reasons it only claims a three nautical mile territorial sea in these straits. This leaves a high seas corridor with no right of transit passage through the straits, although, of course, the waters of the strait are still within the EEZ of Japan. Ships that choose to pass within three nautical miles of the coasts only have the right of innocent passage, and submarines, for example, should travel on the surface.

A problem with transit passage arises with distinguishing a strait used for international navigation. No objective criteria are available to determine the volume and type of traffic required before a strait is accepted as one used for international navigation. The United States takes the position that the test of whether or not a strait is one used for international navigation is principally geographic rather than functional. It is the potential of the strait to be used for international navigation rather than its actual use.[46] The notable example of this problem is the Qiongzhou Strait (Strait of Hainan), which lies entirely within China's claimed territorial sea and internal waters enclosed by straight baselines joining Hainan island to the mainland, but is an important international shipping route carrying traffic between Hong Kong and Haiphong in Vietnam. It is understood, however, that Vietnam does not push the international status of this strait with China.

The straight baseline closing off the eastern entrance to the strait between Hainan and the Chinese mainland is objectionable in view of both its method of drawing and the implications for the freedom of navigation.[47] In any case China has expressed the position that international shipping does not have a right of innocent passage in this strait.[48] Apart from the questionable application of a straight baseline, this position is contrary to both UNCLOS Article 8(2) about a right of innocent passage being preserved in internal waters enclosed by straight baselines that had not previously been considered as such, and UNCLOS Article 35(a), which has the effect of saying that where straight baselines are similarly drawn, the transit passage regime will continue to apply.

Another issue arises because coastal states adjoining a strait used for international navigation have considerable service responsibilities towards vessels passing through the strait – for example, navigational aids, hydrographic charts and other navigational information, search and rescue services, and marine pollution contingency arrangements. However, UNCLOS makes no provision regarding any cost-recovery for these services, and the imposition of a fee for service would amount to denying, hampering or impairing the right of transit passage, contrary to UNCLOS Article 42(2).

Coastal states bordering an international strait have from time to time contemplated compulsory pilotage schemes as part of their ability to control certain aspects of navigation that could impact upon the marine environment.[49] However, with the exception of Torres Strait, such schemes have not been introduced because refusing access to a strait to a vessel on the grounds that it would not accept a pilot would amount to hampering transit passage and be contrary to UNCLOS Article 44 in particular. However, the coastal state may validly make a pilot a condition of entry for those ships that use the strait to enter one of its ports or subsequently pass through its internal waters away from the area of the strait.

Australia was successful, with the concurrence of the International Maritime Organization (IMO), in introducing a compulsory pilotage scheme for parts of the Inner Route in the Great Barrier Reef because this route moves in part through Australia's internal waters.[50] Later in 2005, Australia introduced a compulsory pilotage regime for the Torres Strait that is regarded as a strait used for international navigation.[51] Some considered this move unlawful.[52] A voluntary pilotage regime had previously existed in Torres Strait but as the number of ships not taking a pilot was increasing, and in view of the environmental sensitivity of the region and the hazardous nature of the passage, Australia in conjunction with Papua

New Guinea as the other bordering state to the strait deemed that compulsory pilotage was necessary and persisted with the scheme.

There are several important exceptions to the right of transit passage. First, transit passage is not applicable if the strait does not connect two areas of the high seas or EEZ with one another, as in the case of one leading into the territorial sea or the internal waters of a foreign state.[53] Second, the right of transit passage is excepted in a strait if the strait is formed by an island of a state bordering the strait and its mainland provided 'there exists seaward of the island a route through the high seas or through an exclusive economic zone of similar convenience with respect to navigational and hydrographical characteristics'.[54] Possible examples of this exception in East Asia include the Cheju Strait between the southwestern coast of the Korean Peninsula and Cheju Island,[55] although this matter is the subject of dispute between Japan and South Korea,[56] and Qiongzhou Strait between Hainan and the mainland of China.[57] Third, UNCLOS Article 36 provides that if there is a route through the high seas, or through an EEZ, in a strait that has similar convenience in respect of navigational and hydrographical characteristics, the regime of transit passage is not applicable. If they wish to exercise the freedom of transit passage, then they must use the corridor through the high seas or EEZ.

UNCLOS makes clear that transit passage shall not be hampered or suspended.[58] Ships and aircraft exercising the right of transit passage must 'refrain from any threat or use of force against the sovereignty, territorial integrity or political independence of States bordering the strait'.[59] They must comply with relevant international regulations,[60] as well as with the regulations and laws of the coastal state that can be validly applied to them.[61] However, such regulations and laws must not be discriminatory between different ships and shall not 'in their application have the practical effect of denying, hampering or impairing the right of transit passage'.[62] Thus, while UNCLOS Article 41 allows states bordering straits to designate sea lanes and prescribe traffic separation schemes and Article 42 permits regulations to control and prevent pollution by the discharge of oil, oily wastes and other noxious substances, such regulations cannot operate to deny, hamper or impair the right of transit passage. Both Indonesia and Singapore backed Malaysia's insistence that Japanese plutonium shipments should not be routed through the Malacca Strait.[63]

It has been argued that the issue of international straits has been primarily discussed in political, military and strategic terms and much less in commercial and functional terms.[64]

Churchill and Low agree that a general right of transit passage is not yet established in customary international law.[65] The United States takes a strongly contrary position. It views the right of free transit through international straits and archipelagos as absolutely in accordance with customary law. Such passage is essential for the global mobility of American forces. In the event, for example, that the Strait of Malacca and the straits through the Indonesian archipelago were closed to shipping, a carrier battle group sailing from Yokosuka in Japan to the Persian Gulf would have to re-route around Australia as the draft of its major units would be too deep for them to use the Torres Strait.[66] At a steady speed of 15 knots, the group would require an additional 15 days to transit the additional 5,800 nautical miles.

Malacca and Singapore Straits

The Malacca and Singapore Straits are one of the most important waterways in the world. There were 84,456 transits of the Malacca Straits in 2017 by vessels over 300 gross tons of which 33 per cent were container ships and 29 per cent were tankers, including very large crude carriers (VLCCs).[67] These straits are the most significant in the region where the transit passage regime applies. As the Deputy Prime Minister of Singapore has pointed out, 'transit passage through the Straits of Malacca and Singapore cannot be suspended or impeded, as these waters are crucial to connecting the Pacific and Indian Oceans'.[68]

Implementing the transit passage regime in the Malacca and Singapore Straits has been problematic, particularly with regard to the application of UNCLOS Article 43. This so-called 'burden sharing' article provides for cooperation between user states and states bordering a strait on the provision of navigational and safety aids and the prevention of marine pollution. Over the years, Malaysia has explored various methods of obtaining financial contributions from users of the Malacca Strait to cover the costs of providing services for ships passing through the strait,[69] but user states, other than Japan, have not been prepared to contribute. However, the incidence of piracy and armed robbery against ships in the straits in the early 2000s and the threat of maritime terrorism focussed attention on the extent to which the principles of Article 43 might be extended to cover the security of shipping. In addition to the costs of providing for maritime safety and pollution response, the littoral states have been challenged to increase their patrol and surveillance activities in the straits against the threats of piracy and terrorism.

Japan has been actively involved in measures to ensure the safety of navigation and prevention of marine pollution in the Malacca and Singapore Straits since the late 1960s through the Malacca Strait Council (MSC). The MSC was established in 1969 for the purpose of routine maintenance along the straits. Since then, the MSC has continued its efforts to improve safe navigation and preservation of marine environment in the straits. The work of the MSC is supported by the Japanese Government and maritime private sector. With this funding, the MSC has overseen hydrographic surveys, oil spill countermeasures and the provision of navigational aids in the Malacca Strait.[70] For many years, Japan appeared happy to be the only outside state to contribute to the costs of maintaining these services, but as the costs increased, along with increased use of the straits by other Northeast Asian countries, Japan sought to involve other countries in cost contributions. In doing so, however, it has wanted to maintain its pre-eminent position as the 'lender of first resort'.

Largely as a consequence of Japanese lobbying, a series of meetings sponsored by the IMO was held by the littoral states between 2005 and 2007 to address the issue of burden sharing in straits. The last meeting in Singapore in 2007 agreed the Cooperative Mechanism for Safety of Navigation and Environment Protection in the Straits of Malacca and Singapore.[71] This implements the so-called burden-sharing mechanism in UNCLOS Article 43. Since its inception in 2007, the Co-operative Mechanism has coordinated many projects to promote safety of navigation and environmental protection in the straits.

The Cooperative Mechanism consists of three elements – a Cooperation Forum, an Aids to Navigation Fund, and specific projects.[72] The Cooperation Forum is intended to promote open dialogue and discussions between the littoral states, user states and other stakeholders interested in the safety of navigation in the straits. The Aids to Navigation Fund accepts voluntary contributions from user states and other stakeholders to finance navigational safety and environmental protection by maintaining and replacing aids to navigation such as lighthouses and buoys. Security was not directly included within the remit of the mechanism because Indonesia and Malaysia considered this their sovereign responsibility in their own waters.

The Aids to Navigation Fund was intended to enable user states and other stakeholders to make voluntary contributions for the establishment of navigational aids in the Strait. Unfortunately the required contributions have not been forthcoming with, for example, US$5 million received in 2009 against an annual budget of US$8million, and only US$3.2 million in 2010.[73] Ship-owners and ship-owning associations have not supported the Fund as they regard it as an interference with the freedoms of navigation through a strait used for international navigation. This situation may lead Indonesia and Malaysia to consider stricter measures over shipping passing through the Malacca Strait, including some form of compulsory pilotage and/or by treating the Malacca and Singapore Straits as separate straits with a regime of non-suspendable innocent passage applying to the former.[74] These measures would be strongly opposed by Singapore and major user states, including the United States. The issue remains as to how navigational safety and environmental protection measures will be funded in the longer-term, particularly as shipping traffic increases.

Malaysia and Indonesia have held closely to the principle that security in the Malacca Straits is a matter for the straits' states themselves although Singapore has been more welcoming of outside assistance. Indonesia and Malaysia both strongly opposed the Regional Maritime Security Initiative (RMSI) put forward by the United States in 2004 to provide a conceptual framework for maritime security cooperation in the Malacca Straits.[75] Both countries fastened on the notion that it was an affront to their sovereignty because it may have allowed the positioning of American forces to provide security in the strait. However, both countries have accepted security-related capacity building assistance from the United States on a bilateral basis.

Archipelagic sea lanes passage

UNCLOS established the regime of the archipelagic state that allows states that are constituted wholly of one or more groups of islands and meet certain other criteria specified in the Convention to draw archipelagic baselines joining the outermost islands and drying reefs.[76] With the two largest, and most vocal, archipelagic states in the world, Indonesia and the Philippines, sitting astride major shipping routes between the Indian and Pacific Oceans and East Asia and the Americas and Oceania, the regime of archipelagic sea lanes (ASL) passage is of great strategic importance to the Asia-Pacific region.

The archipelagic state exercises full sovereignty over its archipelagic waters qualified only by ASL passage which allows ships of all nations the right of 'continuous, expeditious and unobstructed transit' through archipelagic waters along sea lanes which may be designated by the archipelagic state.[77] If sea lanes are not designated, then the right of ASL passage may be exercised through the routes normally used for international navigation.[78] Outside these sea lanes, ships of all nations have the right of innocent passage only and must abide by the more restrictive provisions of that regime, including recognition of the principle that the archipelagic state may temporarily suspend innocent passage.[79]

Many of the provisions of UNCLOS relating to transit passage apply also to ASL passage through UNCLOS Article 54, which applies Articles 39, 40, 42 and 44 of the transit passage regime *mutatis mutandis* to archipelagic sea lanes passage. These include the passage of ships in their 'normal modes of continuous and expeditious transit' (Article 39), a prohibition on research or survey activities (Article 40), the laws and regulations of the bordering state relating to passage (Article 42), and the powerlessness of bordering states to hamper or suspend passage (Article 44).

Despite these identical provisions, there are significant differences between the ASL and transit passage regimes. ASL passage is a 'right',[80] whereas transit passage is a 'freedom'.[81] A 'right' implies a more limited entitlement than a 'freedom'. ASL passage is restricted to defined sea lanes within defined limits whereas with transit passage, ships may wander around within the strait, including closely approaching the coast, unless sea lanes or traffic separation schemes have been established. UNCLOS Article 43, the 'burden-sharing' article, does not apply to ASL passage, and whereas transit passage 'shall not be impeded',[82] ASL passage must be 'unobstructed'.[83] Generally ASL principles appear to concede greater control to the archipelagic state than the transit passage principles concede to the states bordering a strait used for international navigation.

Article 53 is the key article of UNCLOS that describes the right of ASL passage. However, it contains several 'grey areas', which could in the future be interpreted more in the favour of archipelagic states. On the issue of designating or substituting sea lanes, or prescribing or substituting traffic separation schemes, an archipelagic state is required to '*refer* proposals to the competent international organisation with a view to their adoption' (emphasis added).[84] The IMO is generally regarded as the appropriate 'competent international organisation', but what is less clear is whether the archipelagic state having referred a proposal to the IMO is then obliged to accept any IMO ruling. 'Referring to' is not the same as 'seeking the approval of', and an archipelagic state may not have to follow the advice of the IMO. It may also be significant that the archipelagic state is required to refer proposals on sea lanes, while it is *in the process* of designating sea lanes,[85] but states adjacent to international straits are required to refer proposals *before* designating sea lanes.[86] While Indonesia has made a partial designation of archipelagic sea lanes, the Philippines, as the other large archipelagic state in the region, has not as yet.

Clearly maritime or *user* states will want to maximise the number of archipelagic sea lanes. On the other hand, archipelagic states wish to minimise this number so as to maximise their potential control over foreign movement within their archipelago, and to limit the freedoms available to foreign ships and aircraft. They are also concerned about issues of marine safety, resource management, and environmental protection associated with the designation of ASLs.

The maritime states base their argument on the unequivocal statement in UNCLOS Article 53(3) that archipelagic sea lanes and air routes 'shall include all normal passage routes used as routes for international navigation or overflight'. However, issues can arise with the identification of which routes may be considered 'normal'. The opposing positions were evident with the United States originally requiring a total of eight sea lanes in the Indonesian archipelago (i.e. five more than then intended by Indonesia) while the United Kingdom required 52![87] The preferred international position may be that sea lanes not be designated at all. There is then full flexibility with regard to selection of routes normally used for international navigation.

The vast difference in operational terms between the liberal nature of the ASL passage regime and the restrictions with innocent passage has made the identification of ASLs a vexed issue. Interpreting the rules for drawing sea lanes, as set out in UNCLOS Article 53(5) in particular, is also proving more complex than may have been anticipated. Technical issues arise with the identification of ASLs requiring detailed work by hydrographers. Continuous axis lines need to be determined from the entry points of each 'normal' passage routes to the exit points. Then the requirement that ships and aircraft in archipelagic sea lanes passage shall not deviate more than 25 nautical miles to either side of such axis lines during passage sets the maximum width of a sea lane at 50 nautical miles, but this is subject to the proviso that ships and aircraft should not navigate closer to the coasts than 10 per cent of the distance between the nearest points on islands along the route or bordering the sea lane. All these technical requirements suggest that the hydrographers and navigational experts of interested parties have to sit down together and go over each potential ASL virtually on a mile by mile basis. This was the experience when Indonesia was in the process of drawing up ASLs.[88]

Indonesia

With Indonesia sitting as it does astride major shipping routes between the Indian and Pacific Oceans, navigational rights and freedoms through Indonesian waters are of great interest both to Indonesia and the international community. However, the vagueness and ambiguity of UNCLOS provisions on navigational regimes and the lack of further guidance on their interpretation and implementation have resulted in different perspectives of these regimes held by Indonesia on the one hand and major maritime powers on the other.[89]

This has been particularly the case with the ASL passage regime. Indonesia's proposal to designate three North/South ASLs in the early 1990s led to detailed analysis and discussion at the IMO,[90] as well as bilateral discussions between Indonesia and interested user states, particularly the United States and Australia.[91] This activity culminated in IMO approval of the 'General Provisions on the Adoption, Designation and Substitution of Archipelagic Sea Lanes' (GPASLs) in 1998.[92] This achieves some balance between the interests of archipelagic states and those of user states.[93]

40 *Navigational regimes*

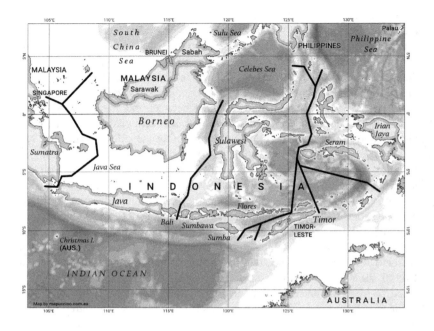

Figure 2.2 Indonesia's archipelagic sea lanes.

The GPASLs include the concept of partial designation of sea lanes to recognise the possibility that in designating ASLs, an archipelagic state may not designate 'all normal passage routes used as routes for international navigation or overflight through or over archipelagic waters'.[94] However, this has been controversial in Indonesia where there is a belief that the concept of partial designation of sea lanes is not in line with UNCLOS Article 53(4), and that it is not within the jurisdiction of the IMO to determine whether all normal routes have been designated or not.[95] That is believed to be a matter for the archipelagic state itself.

Following agreement on GPASLs, there appeared to be an onus on Indonesia to complete the designation process. However, Indonesian Government Regulation No. 37/2002[96] legislates only for the following three North/South ASLs shown in Figure 2.2[97]:

- A lane in the west (ASL Passage I) facilitating navigation from the Indian Ocean through Sunda Strait, Karimata Strait and the Natuna Sea to the South China Sea.

- A central lane (ASL Passage II) for navigation from the Indian Ocean through Lombok and Makassar Straits to the Celebes Sea and the Pacific Ocean.
- A lane in the east (ASL Passage III) with several spurs to facilitate navigation from the Timor and Arafura Seas to the Pacific Ocean via Ombai and Wetar Straits and the Banda, Seram and Molucca Seas.

This regulation does not make clear whether this is a complete or partial designation of sea lanes. While the regulation does not necessarily exclude further ASLs, it does imply that for the time being the right of ASL passage is only available in the designated ASLs and that only innocent passage will apply elsewhere in Indonesia's archipelagic waters. Article 15 of Indonesian Government Regulation 37/2002 'strongly envisages that ships and aircraft may exercise archipelagic sea lanes passage *only* through the designated archipelagic sea lanes'.[98] This reflects the perennial strategic concern of Indonesia that foreign naval and air forces may intentionally pass through or above the waters outside the designated ASLs without conforming to the regime of innocent passage.[99] However, this is contrary to Washington's view that the right of ASL passage may be exercised within the three designated routes, and also within other routes normally used for international navigation, and that any attempts to restrict ASL passage to the designated sea lanes are inconsistent with the navigational rights reflected in UNCLOS.[100]

Another vexed issue with the designation of Indonesian ASLs is the availability of an East–West sea lane through the archipelago via the Java Sea, and linking the three North–South lanes. The user states, Australia in particular, with the regular movement of both merchant vessels and warships through the archipelago from Northwest Australia to Southeast Asia, have been concerned that this ASL should be declared. However, declaration of this sea lane has steadfastly been resisted by Indonesia, mainly due to environmental and security sensitivities with the Java Sea. The Indonesian government has, reportedly on occasion, attempted to restrict the exercise of the right of ASL passage by American military aircraft along east-west routes normally used for international navigation.[101]

A major incident occurred in July 2003 involving the American aircraft carrier USS *Carl Vinson* when two Indonesian F-16Bs intercepted five F/A 18s (Hornets) from the carrier in the Java Sea northwest of Bawean Island (north of Bali) with the aircraft jamming each other's electronics.[102] Indonesia claimed the Hornets were in Indonesian airspace, presumably because they were flying outside of the ASL although the aircraft carrier herself was in an ASL. While the 'rights and wrongs' of this incident are unclear, it does illustrate the operational complexities of implementing the ASL passage for both the archipelagic state and user states.

42 *Navigational regimes*

Philippines

The Republic Act on the Archipelagic Baselines of the Philippines was enacted in 2009 establishing a straight archipelagic baselines system for the Philippines consistent with UNCLOS Article 47.[103] The passing of a new baseline law allowed the Philippines to strengthen its maritime security arrangements, but has not yet led to the designation of ASLs in its archipelago. Figure 2.3 shows the ASLs that were proposed back in 1997.[104] These remain the most likely ones to be designated although nothing definite has been enacted so far. An Act to approve a proposed law providing the parameters for the establishment of the ASLs in the country's archipelagic waters has been before the Philippine House of Representatives for some years but has not yet been approved.[105]

Designating ASLs in the Philippines will likely prove more difficult than for Indonesia. This, along with the practical problems encountered with designating ASLs in Indonesia, suggests the difficulty of applying the general international rules, as embodied in UNCLOS, in the particular geographic, environmental and political contexts of the Philippines.[106] Since no archipelagic sea lanes have been designated in accordance with

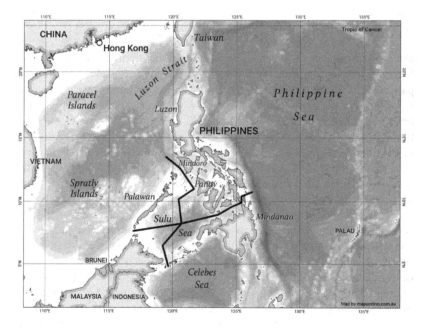

Figure 2.3 Possible Philippine archipelagic sea lanes.

UNCLOS, the 'right of archipelagic sea lane passage may be exercised through the routes normally used for international navigation'.[107]

There are four main reasons why the situation with the Philippines may be even more problematic than that for Indonesia. First, the Philippines generally took a stronger and more inflexible position than Indonesia during negotiations on archipelagic state rights and associated passage regimes when UNCLOS was being formulated.[108] The Philippines consistently argued that the right of innocent passage in archipelagic waters could not be the same as it was in the territorial sea,[109] and that its *archipelagic waters* are in effect *internal waters*.[110] Additionally, the Philippine delegate intervened on several occasions during the negotiations on GPASL at the IMO to indicate that the Indonesian approach was not a precedent for future ASL designations.[111]

Second, the Philippine archipelago is more complex geographically than the Indonesian one with more scattered islands and reefs and less well-defined shipping channels. It will be harder to follow the same process as adopted for Indonesian ASLs with precise determination of the geographical limits of sea lanes. The Philippines has a complex network of inter-island shipping routes with a high incidence of major shipping disasters.[112] The most serious peacetime maritime disaster in the world in terms of loss of life occurred in December 1987 when over 4,300 lives were lost after the inter-island ferry *Dona Paz* caught fire and sank after a collision with an oil tanker, *MT Vector*.[113] Possible ASLs will cross through areas where there are extensive subsistence and commercial fishing operations.

There are serious concerns about the state of the marine environment of the Philippines. The dangers of ship-sourced marine pollution are likely to lead the Philippines to assert strict controls over the passage of shipping through its archipelago. The arguments by the United States for freedoms of navigation for warships in archipelagic waters were not helped when the minesweeper USS *Guardian* was wrecked in January 2013 on an environmentally sensitive reef in Philippine archipelagic waters in the Sulu Sea that was a marine sanctuary protected as a Philippine National Marine Park, and declared as a World Heritage Site by UNESCO.[114] Human error was likely a major cause of this accident exacerbated by the *Guardian* apparently ignoring warnings from park rangers that she was approaching the reef. The Philippines received nearly US$2 million from the United States in compensation for the environmental damage caused by this grounding.[115] The *Guardian* had to be cut to pieces to avoid further damage to the World Heritage site in a salvage operation that took ten weeks.

Third, the Philippine archipelago sits astride major shipping routes between the Americas and southern China and Southeast Asia, as well as between northern Australia and the Lombok Strait and Northeast Asia. The narrowness of some straits highlights the potential difficulties in developing axis lines and applying the 10 per cent rule in UNCLOS Article 53(5). Other international shipping routes lie immediately to the North of the Philippines through the Luzon Strait between Taiwan and the Philippines, and to the South between Mindanao and Indonesia. Parts of these routes pass through Philippine archipelagic waters.

Lastly, there is the political problem in the Philippines with the Treaty of Paris limits and the so-called 'picture frame' territorial sea around the Philippine archipelago.[116] On signing UNCLOS, the Philippines made a declaration that such signing did not affect the sovereign rights of the Philippines under the Treaty of Paris, and that 'the concept of archipelagic waters is similar to the concept of internal waters under the Constitution of the Philippines'.[117] The 2009 Philippines archipelagic baselines legislation did not clarify whether the waters within the baselines are archipelagic waters or internal waters.[118] The Treaty of Paris limits are locked into Philippine public policy and it is unlikely that any Philippine politician or Minister would propose that they formally be renounced.

Instead of looking at the various regimes in a segmented way (e.g. transit passage and ASL passage), there might be merit in taking a holistic view of the need to ensure a consistent approach to navigation through the East Asian seas rather than one that depends on the vagaries of individual coastal and archipelagic states.[119] A seamless maritime transit architecture involving the Straits of Malacca and Singapore and the ASLs of Indonesia and the Philippines might be possible. Certainly there would seem to be a need for some consistency between the two large archipelagic states, Indonesia and the Philippines.

Normal mode of transit

The mode of transit adopted by ships and aircraft exercising transit and ASL passage is another difficult issue with implementing the UNCLOS navigational regimes in the region. Ships and aircraft exercising the freedom of transit passage are required to 'refrain from any activities other than those incident to their normal modes of continuous and expeditious transit'.[120] Similarly, ASL passage means the exercise 'of the rights of navigation and overflight in the normal mode'.[121] But what is the normal mode of transit for a ship, submarine or aircraft?

It is generally accepted that the normal mode of transit for submarines is submerged. However, safety concerns have been raised about submarines transiting the Philippine archipelago submerged due to the risk of their getting caught up in the fishing nets or fish aggregating devices that are used extensively in Philippine archipelagic waters.[122] The types of operation that might be conducted by transiting ships and aircraft are also problematic. Surface vessels may adopt a tactical disposition, operating aircraft and conducting non-delaying exercises, but what are the limits for example on the defensive screens, evasive tactics, air cover and so on that might be used by a naval task force exercising the right of ASL passage and could take unites outside the ASL? Indonesian Government Regulation No. 37/2002 declares that 'when exercising right of Archipelagic Sea Lane Passage, foreign military and warships must not conduct military exercises or exercise any type of weapons with ammunition'.[123] However, the maritime powers would view exercising as part of the normal mode of warship transit.

Unsurprisingly, incidents have occurred over the years associated with the transit of warships through the Indonesian archipelago. Mainly these have involved aircraft. Organic aircraft should remain within the designated sea lane and not fly beyond 25 nautical miles to either side of the axis line during passage. For example, the 'cross-decking' of a helicopter from a ship in one ASL to a ship in another ASL may not be permissible when no right of overflight exists outside an ASL.

Submarine operations

With the proliferation of submarines in the region, including in the South China Sea,[124] the provisions of the navigational regimes in UNCLOS related to submarine operations, particularly those conducted in coastal waters, need to be considered.[125] The innocent passage regime places specific restrictions on warships exercising the right of innocent passage through the territorial sea of another state, including that submarines should transit on the surface and show their flag.[126] It is possible, however, that due to the very nature of submarine operations, this provision is honoured more in its breach rather than in its observance except in circumstances when navigational conditions, particularly water depth, require that the submarine should travel on the surface.

Special rules relate to the passage of submarines through the waters of an archipelagic state, such as Indonesia or the Philippines, or through a strait used for international navigation, such as the straits of Malacca or Hormuz. It is generally accepted that where navigational conditions permit, submarines can travel submerged through these waters in accordance with the 'normal mode' provisions of the straits' transit passage[127] and archipelagic sea lanes passage[128] regimes in UNCLOS. However, in archipelagic waters outside of archipelagic sea lanes or routes normally used for international navigation, submarines should conform to the much more restrictive innocent passage regime and travel on the surface.

Indonesia is very concerned about possible breaches of its sovereignty in its archipelagic waters.[129] It is particularly sensitive to the movement of foreign warships and submarines through these waters, especially the possibility of submarines travelling submerged outside of its declared archipelagic sea lanes. There have been several incidents over the years in Indonesian waters, involving Australian or American submarines, where Indonesia has queried submarine movements in its archipelagic waters. In 2000, President Wahid warned Singapore not to allow its submarines to stray into Indonesian waters, promising a swift military response should that occur.[130] The Indonesian Navy claims to have often detected submarines shadowing its naval exercises.[131]

The implication of the articles of UNCLOS dealing with innocent passage in the territorial sea is that submerged passage in the territorial sea, or in archipelagic waters outside of archipelagic sea lanes, is not innocent passage and may be prevented by force. However, it is not as easy as that. The law relating to the innocent passage of submarines can be 'a dangerous weapon to both sides' (i.e. to the flag state of the submarine and to the coastal state involved).[132] To say that it is non-innocent passage when a submarine breaches its duty to remain on the surface in the territorial sea (or archipelagic waters) of another state is rather like saying that exceeding the speed limit on a road makes the purpose of the journey illegal.[133]

The reasonableness or otherwise of the submarine travelling submerged needs to be judged against the circumstances of each case. Relevant factors might include 'the weather conditions at the time, the political climate, and, most important, the track taken by the submarine'.[134] The submarine's track is an important factor because this might be 'continuous and expeditious' within the meaning of the innocent passage regime,[135] or the submarine might be loitering or have diverted into the territorial sea perhaps to gather intelligence in which cases the passage could be deemed non-innocent. These are important issues for East Asia where countries may want to have their submarines transiting submerged through the territorial sea or archipelagic waters of another, or may send their submarines into these waters for covert intelligence collection or surveillance purposes.

Conclusion

As discussed in this chapter, several 'grey areas' remain with the transit and ASL passage regimes in UNCLOS. These regimes are important in the Asia-Pacific yet they are great areas of residual uncertainty as far as navigational issues are concerned. A workshop on international navigation aspects of the law of the sea held in Honolulu back in 1986 identified them as 'still unresolved issues' along with the rights of innocent passage of naval vessels through territorial waters without prior notification.[136] Little has happened since them to resolve these difficulties and if anything, the conflicts of interest are now even more acute.

The regimes of ASL and transit passage and overflight are of prime interest to warships and military aircraft. Overflight is available under these regimes to military aircraft and naval vessels can travel *in the normal mode*. It may be argued that the interests of commercial shipping are met sufficiently by the innocent passage regime, and commercial aircraft operate under international civil aviation rules. However, there is still the key distinction that innocent passage may be suspended in particular areas for particular periods of time. Also, the arbitrary ability of an archipelagic state to prevent commercial traffic from using routes outside of ASLs could have serious economic penalties. It would also be contrary to the spirit of the *quid pro quo* involved with international acceptance of the archipelagic state regime that the archipelagic state should not impose itself as a major (or impenetrable) barrier to normal shipping traffic.

States adjacent to major international straits or archipelagic states with major shipping routes passing through their archipelagic waters will likely seek a greater degree of control over transiting vessels primarily on environmental grounds. Frequently, though, the environmental concerns may be the 'cloak' for other reasons to regulate the movement of shipping including for reasons of national security. It is all too easy to place new restrictions on freedoms of navigation, but a line may have to be drawn eventually. All states benefit from the unimpeded movement of merchant ships and their cargoes. There is no provision in UNCLOS for the payment of 'tolls' to exercise navigational rights and freedoms and the failure of shipping nations to share the burden of costs associated with maintaining navigational safety in straits and archipelagic waters could well lead to a more assertive approach by straits and archipelagic states.[137]

Notes

1 *Convention on Territorial Sea and the Contiguous Zone.* Done at Geneva on 29 April 1958. Entered into force on 10 September 1964, United Nations, *Treaty Series*, Vol. 516, p. 205. Article 14(4) of this convention simply provides that 'Passage is innocent so long as it is not prejudicial to the peace, good order or security of the coastal State' without further amplification other than the limitations in Article 14(5) about fishing vessels not fishing, and in Article 14(6) that 'Submarines are required to navigate on the surface and to show their flag'.
2 UNCLOS Article 25(3).
3 UNCLOS Article 20.
4 UNCLOS Article 19(2)(e).
5 UNCLOS Article 19(2)(j).

48 *Navigational regimes*

6 Unimpeded passage through straits used for international navigation and ASL passage became linked at the 3rd Session of UNCLOS III as the *quid pro quo* for the seabed mining regime in UNCLOS Part XI and the EEZ regime. Edward L. Miles, *Global Ocean Politics – The Decision Process at the Third United Nations Conference on the Law of the Sea 1973–1982*, The Hague: Martinus Nijhoff Publishers, 1998, p. 52.
7 UNCLOS Article 8(2).
8 Based on data from US Navy Judge Advocate General's Corp, *Maritime Claims Reference Manual*, www.jag.navy.mil/organization/code_10_mcrm.htm.
9 Yoshifumi Tanaka, 'Navigational Rights and Freedoms' in Donald R. Rothwell, Alex G. Oude Elferink, Karen N. Scott and Tim Stephens (eds), *The Oxford Handbook of the Law of the Sea*, Oxford: Oxford University Press, 2015, p. 545.
10 J. Ashley Roach and Robert W. Smith, 'Excessive Maritime Claims' in *International Law Studies*, Vol. 66, Newport R.I.: USN War College, 1994, Table 10, pp. 158–159. The current *Maritime Claims Reference Manual* suggests Cambodia and the Philippines do not have a requirement for prior notification but there is no indication that the requirement recorded by Roach and Smith has been rescinded.
11 United Nations, *The Law of the Sea: Declarations and Statements with Respect to the United Nations Convention on the Law of the Sea and to the Agreement Relating to the Implementation of Part XI of the United Nations Convention on the Law of the Sea*, (United Nations publication, Sales No. E.97.V.3). See also, Zou Keyuan, 'Innocent Passage for Warships: The Chinese Doctrine and Practice', *Ocean Development and International Law*, Vol. 29, 1998, p. 201.
12 Kresno Buntoro, *An analysis of legal issues relating to navigational rights and freedoms through and over Indonesian waters*, PhD thesis, University of Wollongong, 2010, http://ro.uow.edu.au/theses/3091, pp. 95–96.
13 As quoted in Roach and Smith, *Excessive Maritime Claims*, p. 156.
14 Tanaka, 'Navigational Rights and Freedoms', p. 547.
15 Sam Bateman, 'Solving the "Wicked Problems" of Maritime Security – Are Regional Forums up to the Task?', *Contemporary Southeast Asia*, Vol. 33, No. 1, 2011, pp. 1–28.
16 UNCLOS Article 21.
17 UNCLOS Article 24(1)(a).
18 UNCLOS Article 25.
19 Donald R. Rothwell, 'Coastal State Sovereignty and Innocent Passage: The Voyage of the Lusitania Expresso', *Marine Policy*, Vol. 16, 1992, p. 427.
20 David F. Froman, 'Uncharted Waters: Non-Innocent Passage of Warships in the Territorial Sea', *San Diego Law Review*, Vol. 21, No. 3, June 1984, p. 658.
21 UNCLOS Article 19(2)(c).
22 Francis Ngantcha, *The Right of Innocent Passage and the Evolution of the International Law of the Sea*, London: Pinter, 1990, p. 131.
23 Froman, 'Uncharted Waters', especially pp. 651–652 and pp. 688–689.
24 Tanaka, 'Navigational Rights and Freedoms', p. 547.
25 Tullio Scovazzi, 'Management Regimes and Responsibility for International Straits', *MIMA Issue Paper*, undated, p. 11.

Navigational regimes 49

26 R.R. Churchill and A.V. Lowe, *The Law of the Sea*, Manchester: Juris Publishing, Manchester University Press, 3rd. edn, 1999, p. 90.
27 Zou, 'Innocent Passage for Warships'.
28 Ngantcha, *The Right of Innocent Passage*, p. 149.
29 Churchill and Lowe, *The Law of the Sea*, p. 90.
30 Sam Bateman, 'Maritime Confidence and Security Building Measures in the Asian Pacific Region and the Law of the Sea' in James Crawford and Donald R. Rothwell (eds), *The Law of the Sea in the Asian Pacific Region*, Dordrecht: Martinus Nijhoff, 1995, pp. 223–236.
31 The use of straight baselines in East Asia is comprehensively discussed in: Sam Bateman and Clive Schofield, 'State Practice Regarding Straight Baselines in East Asia – Legal, Technical and Political Issues in a Changing Environment', Paper presented at international conference on *Difficulties in Implementing the Provisions of UNCLOS*, International Hydrographic Bureau, Monaco, 16–17 October 2008 (available online at: www.iho.int/mtg_docs/com_wg/ABLOS/ABLOS_Conf5/Papers/Session7-Paper1-Bateman.pdf).
32 US Department of State, Bureau of Oceans and Environmental and Scientific Affairs, 'Straight Baseline Claim: China', *Limits in the Seas, No. 117*, 1996, www.state.gov/documents/organization/57692.pdf, p. 3.
33 Kriangsak Kittichaisaree, *The Law of the Sea and Maritime Boundary Delimitation in South-East Asia*, Singapore: Oxford University Press, 1987, pp. 17–18.
34 For a comprehensive description of the US response to straight baseline systems, see J. Ashley Roach and Robert W. Smith, 'Straight Baselines: The Need for a Universally Applied Norm', *Ocean Development and International Law*, Vol. 31, 2000, pp. 47–80.
35 Kriangsak, *The Law of the Sea and Maritime Boundary Delimitation*, p. 16.
36 Based on US State Department, 'Vietnam – Straight Baselines', *Limits in the Seas No. 99*, 12 December 1983.
37 UNCLOS Article 7(1).
38 Article 27(1), The Law of the Sea of Vietnam, *Vietnam News*, https://vietnamnews.vn/politics-laws/228456/the-law-of-the-sea-of-viet-nam.html#LQYW35Rk2IqyO5R2.97.
39 Article 12(2), The Law of the Sea of Vietnam.
40 Du Viet Cuong, 'Vietnam's South China Sea Approach after National Congress', *Asia Maritime Transparency Initiative*, 27 February 2016, https://amti.csis.org/vietnam-scs-approach/.
41 For a description of the development of this regime see Donald R. Rothwell, 'International Straits and UNCLOS: An Australian Case Study', *Journal of Maritime Law and Commerce*, Vol. 23, No. 3, 1992, pp. 461–483.
42 Lewis M. Alexander, 'Exceptions to the Transit Passage Regime: Straits with Routes of "Similar Convenience"', *Ocean Development and International Law*, Vol. 18, No. 4, 1987, pp. 480–481.
43 UNCLOS Article 38(2).
44 Ibid.
45 US Department of Defense, *National Security and the Convention on the Law of the Sea*, 2nd edn, 1996, p. 5.
46 James Kraska, *Maritime Power and the Law of the Sea*, New York: Oxford University Press, 2011, p. 126.
47 US Department of State, 'Straight Baseline Claim: China'.

50 *Navigational regimes*

48 Chen Degong, 'China and the Law of the Sea', *Occasional Paper*, Canberra, Northeast Asia Program, Research School of Pacific and Asian Studies, Australian National University, December 1996, p. 17.
49 Rothwell, 'Navigational Rights and Freedoms', pp. 604–607.
50 Ibid.
51 Sam Bateman, 'Compulsory Pilotage in the Torres Strait' in Andrew Forbes (ed.), *Australian Maritime Issues 2007*, Papers in Australian Maritime Affairs No. 21, Canberra: Sea Power Centre – Australia, 2008, pp. 183–187.
52 Robert Beckman, 'Australia's Pilotage System in the Torres Strait: A Threat to Transit Passage?', *IDSS Commentary 125/2006*, Singapore: Institute of Defence and Strategic Studies, 7 December 2006.
53 A strait leading from a part of the high seas or an exclusive economic zone into the territorial sea of a foreign state is subject under UNCLOS Article 45 to the regime of non-suspendable innocent passage. Obviously, passage from the high seas or an EEZ into the internal waters of a state can be suspended.
54 UNCLOS Article 38.
55 Dalchoong Kim and Jin-Hyun Paik, 'The Relation between User States and Coastal States with Respect to International Navigation' in T. Kuribayashi and E.L. Miles (eds), *The Law of the Sea in the 1990s: A Framework for Further International Cooperation*, Honolulu: Law of the Sea Institute, University of Hawaii, 1992, p. 62.
56 Ivan Shearer, 'Navigation Issues in the Asian Pacific Region' in James Crawford and Donald R. Rothwell (eds), *The Law of the Sea in the Asian Pacific Region*, Dordrecht: Martinus Nijhoff, 1995, p. 215.
57 Farhad Talaie, 'Analysis of the Provisions of the LOSC on the Exceptions to the Rights of Transit Passage through International Straits and Related Issues', *Maritime Studies*, 100, May/June 1998, p. 18.
58 UNCLOS Article 44.
59 UNCLOS Article 39(1)(b).
60 UNCLOS Articles 39(2) and (3).
61 UNCLOS Article 42(4).
62 UNCLOS Article 42(2).
63 Jon M. Van Dyke, 'Sea Shipment of Japanese Plutonium under International Law', *Ocean Development and International Law*, Vol. 24, 1993, pp. 399–403.
64 Edgar Gold, 'Transit Services in International Straits: Towards Shared Responsibilities', *MIMA Issue Paper*, Kuala Lumpur, Malaysian Institute of Maritime Affairs, 1995.
65 Churchill and Lowe, *The Law of the Sea*, p. 113.
66 US Department of Defense, *National Security and the Convention on the Law of the Sea*, Figure 4, p. 10.
67 Marcus Hand, 'Malacca Straits VLCC Traffic Doubles in a Decade as Shipping Traffic Hits All Time High in 2017', *Seatrade Maritime News*, 19 February 2018, www.seatrade-maritime.com/news/asia/exclusive-malacca-straits-vlcc-traffic-doubles-in-a-decade-as-shipping-traffic-hits-all-time-high-in-2017.html.
68 'Keeping Straits of Malacca and Singapore Open to Shipping Key to Success of Maritime Silk Road, says DPM Teo', *Straits Times*, 13 July 2017, www.straitstimes.com/singapore/keeping-straits-of-malacca-open-to-shipping-key-to-success-of-maritime-silk-road-says-dpm.

69 Alternative methods of covering the costs are explored in various papers in Hamzah bin Ahmad (ed.), *The Straits of Malacca: International Cooperation in Trade, Funding and Navigational Safety*, Kuala Lumpur: Pelanduk, 1997.
70 Tetsuo Kotani, 'Japan's maritime challenges and priorities', Chapter 12 *in* Joshua Ho and Sam Bateman (eds), *Maritime Challenges and Priorities in Asia – Implications for Regional Security*, Abingdon: Routledge, 2012, p. 208.
71 Robert Beckman, 'Maritime Security and the Cooperative Mechanism for the Straits of Malacca and Singapore' in Sam Bateman and Joshua Ho (eds), *Southeast Asia and the Rise of Chinese and Indian Naval Power – Between Rising Naval Powers*. Routledge, Abingdon, 2010, pp. 114–128.
72 Cooperative Mechanism portal www.cm-soms.com/?p=td&id=7.
73 Mohd Hazmi bin Mohd Rusli, 'The Application of Compulsory Pilotage in Straits Used for International Navigation: A Study of the Straits of Malacca and Singapore', *Asian Politics & Policy*, Vol. 3, No. 4, October 2011, p. 508.
74 See arguments in Rusli, 'The Application of Compulsory Pilotage'.
75 Victor Huang, 'Building Maritime Security in Southeast Asia – Outsiders Not Welcome?' *Naval War College Review*, Vol. 61, No. 1, Winter, 2008, p. 93.
76 The provisions of the archipelagic state regime are provided in UNCLOS Part IV.
77 UNCLOS Article 53 (1), (2) and (3). Archipelagic sea lanes should not be confused with the sea lanes and traffic separation schemes that coast state may designate or prescribe for the regulation of the passage of ships though its territorial sea in accordance with UNCLOS Article 22.
78 UNCLOS Article 53 (12).
79 UNCLOS Article 52 (2).
80 UNCLOS Article 38(2) states

> Transit passage means the exercise in accordance with this Part of the freedom of navigation and overflight solely for the purpose of continuous and expeditious transit of the strait between one part of the high seas or an exclusive economic zone and another part of the high seas or an exclusive economic zone.

81 UNCLOS Article 53(3) states

> Archipelagic sea lanes passage means the exercise in accordance with this Convention of the rights of navigation and overflight in the normal mode solely for the purpose of continuous, expeditious and unobstructed transit between one part of the high seas or an exclusive economic zone and another part of the high seas or an exclusive economic zone.

82 UNCLOS Article 38(1).
83 UNCLOS Article 53(3).
84 UNCLOS Article 53(9).
85 UNCLOS Article 53(9).
86 UNCLOS Article 41(4)).
87 Rear Admiral R.M. Sunardi, Comments at a conference on 'Indonesia', 20th National Conference of Australian Institute of International Affairs, Canberra, 25–26 November 1994.
88 Robin Warner, 'Implementing the Archipelagic Regime in the International Maritime Organization' in Donald Rothwell and Sam Bateman (eds), *Navigational Rights and Freedoms and the New Law of the Sea*, The Hague: Martinus Nijhoff Publishers, 2000, pp. 170–171.

89 Buntoro, *An Analysis of Legal Issues Relating to Navigational Rights and Freedoms through and over Indonesian Waters*, p. v.
90 Indonesia's process of designating sea lanes is described in detail in Buntoro, *An Analysis of Legal Issues Relating to Navigational Rights and Freedoms through and over Indonesian Waters*, pp. 133–145. See also, C. Johnson, 'A Rite of Passage: The IMO Consideration of the Indonesian Archipelagic Sea-Lanes Submission', *The International Journal of Marine and Coastal Law*, Vol. 15, No. 3, August 2000, pp. 317–332.
91 Robin Warner, 'Implementing the Archipelagic Regime', pp. 170–171.
92 Indonesia's proposal to designate three North/South archipelagic sea lanes (ASLs) and the General Provisions on the Adoption, Designation and Substitution of Archipelagic Sea Lanes (GPASL) were adopted at the 69th meeting of the IMO's Maritime Safety Committee (MSC) in May 1998. GPASL form part of the IMO Ships Routeing Publication.
93 Masitha Tismananda Kumala and Dina Sunyowati, 'Designation of Archipelagic Sea Lanes According to The United Nations Convention on The Law of the Sea 1982 (Indonesia Archipelagic Sea Lanes Case)', *International Journal of Business, Economics and Law*, Vol. 10, No. 4, August 2016, and Buntoro, *An Analysis of Legal Issues Relating to Navigational Rights and Freedoms through and over Indonesian Waters*, p. 140.
94 UNCLOS Article 53(4).
95 Buntoro, *An Analysis of Legal Issues Relating to Navigational Rights and Freedoms through and over Indonesian Waters*, p. 141.
96 Indonesian Government Regulation No. 37/2002, Relating to Rights and Obligations of Foreign Ships and Aircraft when exercising Rights of Archipelagic Sea Lane Passage via the Established Archipelagic Sea Lanes, enacted by the President of the Republic of Indonesia in Jakarta, 28 June 2002. Reprinted in: UN Division for Ocean Affairs and the Law of the Sea, Office of Legal Affairs, *Law of the Sea Bulletin No. 52*, New York: United Nations, 2003, pp. 20–40, www.un.org/Depts/los/doalos_publications/LOSBulletins/bulletinpdf/bulletin52e.pdf.
97 Based on Indonesian Government Regulation Number 37 2002, 28 June 2002, as reprinted in US State Department, 'Indonesia's Maritime Claims and Boundaries', *Limits in the Seas No. 141*, 16 September 2014.
98 Dhiana Puspitawati, 'The East/West Archipelagic Sea Lanes Passage through the Indonesian Archipelago', *Maritime Studies 140*, January/February 2005, p. 7.
99 Evan A. Laksmana and Ristian A. Supriyanto, 'Abandoned at Sea: The Tribunal Ruling and Indonesia's Missing Archipelagic Foreign Policy', *Asian Politics & Policy*, Vol. 10, No. 2, 2018, p. 311.
100 US Department of State, Office of Ocean and Polar Affairs, Bureau of Oceans and International Environmental and Scientific Affairs, 'Indonesia – Archipelagic and Other Maritime Claims and Boundaries', *Limits in the Seas*, No. 141, 15 September 2014, p. 5, www.state.gov/documents/organization/231912.pdf.
101 Ibid.
102 This incident is described in Buntoro, *An Analysis of Legal Issues Relating to Navigational Rights and Freedoms through and over Indonesian Waters*, pp. 186–188.
103 Mary Ann Palma, 'Maintaining Good Order at Sea – Maritime Challenges and Priorities in the Philippines', Chapter 7 in Joshua Ho and Sam Bateman

(eds), *Maritime Challenges and Priorities in Asia – Implications for Regional Security*, Abingdon: Routledge, 2012, p. 116.
104 Figure 2.3 is based on: Source: Mario Manansala, 'Designation of Archipelagic Sea Lanes in the Philippines' in Maribel B. Aquilos, 'Issue Focus: Designation of Sea Lanes in the Philippines', *Ocean Law and Policy Series*, Vol. 1, No. 1, January–June 1997, p. 10.
105 Senate of the Philippines, 17th Congress, *Philippine Archipelagic Sea Lanes Act*, Senate Bill No. 92. Filed on June 30, 2016 by Trillanes, Antonio 'Sonny' F., www.senate.gov.ph/lis/bill_res.aspx?congress=17&q=SBN-92.
106 These contexts are discussed comprehensively in Mary Ann Palma, 'The Philippines as an Archipelagic and Maritime Nation', *RSIS Working Paper 182*, 21 July 2009, www.rsis.edu.sg/wp-content/uploads/rsis-pubs/WP182.pdf.
107 UNCLOS Article 53 (12).
108 Samuel Soriano, 'Negotiating History of the Archipelagic Passage' in Maribel B. Aquilos, 'Issue Focus: Designation of Sea Lanes in the Philippines', *Ocean Law and Policy Series*, Vol. 1, No. 1, January–June 1997, p. 68.
109 Barbara Kwiatkowska and Etty R. Agoes, *Archipelagic State Regime in the Light of the 1982 UNCLOS and State Practice*, Netherlands Cooperation with Indonesia in Legal Matters, Bandung: ICLOS, UNPAD, April, 1991, p. 19; and Jay L. Batongbacal, 'A Philippine Perspective on Archipelagic State issues', *Maritime Studies*, 122, January–February 2002, pp. 20–21.
110 Tomas Aquino, 'Implications of Sea Lanes Designation on Safety of Navigation and Sovereignty Issues' in Aquilos, 'Issue Focus: Designation of Sea Lanes in the Philippines', p. 15.
111 Warner, 'Implementing the Archipelagic Regime', p. 187.
112 Palma, 'Maintaining Good Order at Sea', pp. 118–119.
113 Joey A. Gabieta, 'Doña Paz Victims Waiting for Justice 25 Years After', *Philippine Daily Inquirer*, 20 December 2012, https://newsinfo.inquirer.net/327123/dona-paz-victims-waiting-for-justice-25-years-after.
114 Sam Bateman, 'Grounding of USS *Guardian* in Philippines: Longer-term Implications', *East Asia Forum*, 9 March 2013, www.eastasiaforum.org/2013/03/09/grounding-of-uss-guardian-in-the-philippines-longer-term-implications/#comments).
115 'US pays Philippines $2m compensation for Damage Caused to Tubbataha Reef by Warship USS *Guardian*', *ABC News*, 18 February 2015, www.abc.net.au/news/2015-02-18/us-pays-philippines-compensation-for-warship-reef-damage/6143302.
116 Signed by Spain and the United States on 10 December 1898. This is the basis of the Philippine 'picture frame' claim to territorial sea. This 'picture frame' purports to describe the area of land and water under the sovereign jurisdiction of the Philippines.
117 United Nations, *The Law of the Sea: Declarations and statements with respect to the United Nations Convention on the Law of the Sea and to the Agreement relating to the Implementation of Part XI of the United Nations Convention on the Law of the Sea* (United Nations publication, Sales No. E.97.V.3).
118 US Department of State, 'Philippines: Archipelagic and other Maritime Claims and Boundaries', *Limits in the Seas*, No. 142, 15 September 2014, p. 4.
119 Hon. Domingo Siazon Jnr., Keynote Address published in Douglas M. Johnston and Ankana Sirivivatnanon (eds), *Maritime Transit and Port State*

54 *Navigational regimes*

      Control: Trends in System Compliance, Bangkok: Southeast Asian Programme in Ocean Law, Policy and Management (SEAPOL), 2000, p. 9.
120 UNCLOS Article 39(1)(c).
121 UNCLOS Article 53(3).
122 Batongbacal, 'A Philippine Perspective on Archipelagic State Issues', p. 27.
123 Indonesian Government Regulation No. 37/2002 Article 4(4).
124 Five of the seven claimant countries in the South China Sea operate submarines. Tyler Headley, 'Submarines in the South China Sea Conflict', *The Diplomat*, 10 August 2018, https://thediplomat.com/2018/08/submarines-in-the-south-china-sea-conflict/. The dangers of submarine proliferation in the region more generally are discussed in Sam Bateman, 'Perils of the Deep – The Dangers of Submarine Proliferation in the Seas of East Asia', *Asian Security*, Vol. 7, No. 1, 2011, pp. 61–84.
125 Relevant issues are discussed extensively in James Kraska, 'Putting Your Head in the Tiger's Mouth: Submarine Espionage in Territorial Waters', *Columbia Journal of Transnational Law*, 54, 2015, pp. 164–247.
126 UNCLOS Article 20.
127 UNCLOS Part III Section 2.
128 UNCLOS Article 53.
129 Archipelagic waters are those within archipelagic baselines around the outermost limits of the archipelago drawn in accordance with Article 47 of UNCLOS. Archipelagic waters come under full sovereignty of the archipelagic state with the exceptions of the rights of innocent passage and archipelagic sea lanes passage.
130 'Wahid Warns Singapore Submarines Not to Stray', *Reuters News*, 26 April 2000.
131 'TNI Navy Training is Shadowed by Foreign Submarine', *TEMP Interactive*, 14 December 2005, www.tempointeractive.com/hg/nasional/2005/12/14/brk,20051214-70643,uk.html.
132 D.P. O'Connell, *The Influence of Law on Sea Power*, Annapolis: Naval Institute Press, 1975, p. 142.
133 Ibid.
134 Ibid., p. 143.
135 UNCLOS Article 18(2).
136 J.P.L. Fonteyne, 'Review of International Navigation: Rocks and Shoals Ahead', *Maritime Studies No. 48*, September/October 1989, p. 8. This is a summary of an annual conference of the Law of the Sea Institute the full proceedings of which were published in Jon Van Dyke, Lewis M. Alexander and Joseph R. Morgan (eds), *International Navigation: Rocks and Shoals Ahead?*, Honolulu: Law of the Sea Institute, University of Hawaii, 1988.
137 Sergei Vinogradov, 'Tightening the Regulatory Web: Issues and Trends in Navigation Regimes' in D. Vidas and W. Ostreng (eds), *Order for the Oceans at the Turn of the Century*, Dordrecht: The Fridtjof Nansen Institute, 1999, p. 480.

3 Exclusive economic zone issues

Introduction

The EEZ regime is covered in Part V of UNCLOS. It gives coastal states sovereign rights for the purposes of exploring, exploiting, conserving and managing the living and non-living resources of the water column, seabed and subsoil to a maximum distance of 200 nautical miles from the baselines from which the breadth of the territorial sea is measured.[1] It also grants the coastal state jurisdiction with regard to the establishment and use of artificial islands, installations and structures; marine scientific research; and the protection and preservation of the marine environment.[2]

Introduction of the EEZ regime brought about one-third of the world's oceans under a form of national jurisdiction. Island states and countries with island territories were the big 'winners' with the regime. Even a small isolated feature in the ocean, which is more than 200 nautical miles from any other feature and meets the UNCLOS definition of an 'island', potentially can generate an EEZ of over 125,600 square nautical miles or 430,800 square kilometres. In view of the extent of this jurisdiction, controversy can arise with applying the regime of islands in UNCLOS Article 121 with regard to determining what is an 'island' entitled to a full suite of maritime zones and what is just a 'rock' entitled only to a territorial sea.[3]

Development of the EEZ regime

The EEZ was a new development in the international law of the sea introduced by UNCLOS, and aspects of this regime are still evolving.[4] The idea of the EEZ had its origins in the move by many states, mainly less developed ones, in the 1950s and 1960s to establish 'fishing zones' in their offshore waters to gain greater control over management of their offshore resources and to restrict access by foreign fishing vessels. Initially the idea of a resource zone was widely supported, including by the maritime powers, because it was assumed that such a zone would not impact on high seas freedoms of navigation and that benefits would accrue from more effective management of resources and protection of the marine environment.[5]

Negotiation of the EEZ regime at the Third UN Conference on the Law of the Sea (UNCLOS III) was difficult and complex with divergent points of view about the status of the new zone. One major group, the 'territorialists', mainly comprising developing countries, saw the EEZ as an extension of national jurisdiction in which the coastal states would enjoy sovereignty subject to certain limitations. However, this position was sharply disputed by the maritime powers, led by the United States and the then Soviet Union, who saw the zone as a part of the high seas where coastal states had some rights over offshore resources but where all the high seas freedoms of navigation and overflight would also apply. The compromise reached was that the EEZ should be regarded as a separate zone in its own right (*sui generis*) neither high seas nor territorial sea with its own distinctive legal regime as set out in UNCLOS Part V.[6]

This compromise has led to disagreements and misunderstandings over the freedoms of navigation available in an EEZ. An important area of disagreement relates to the ability of a coastal state to introduce regulations that have the effect of denying freedoms of navigation and overflight in all or part of its EEZ. The maritime powers argue that, subject to the resource-related rights and environmental protection obligations of a coastal state, the freedoms of navigation and overflight in the EEZ are the same as those on the high seas.[7] This is without requiring prior notice to or authorisation from, the coastal state.[8]

With respect to military uses of the EEZ, the Convention does not make clear whether military activities are included in the freedoms of navigation and overflight and other internationally lawful uses of the sea available under Articles 58 and 87 of UNCLOS.[9] Without having to list explicitly their military rights within the EEZ, the maritime powers sought to ensure during UNCLOS III negotiations that the new EEZ regime would not exclude naval operations in the zone. This led to the 'Castaneda Compromise' put together by the so-called Castaneda Group during negotiations on the legal status of the EEZ at UNCLOS III.[10]

The Castaneda Compromise produced the somewhat over-stated but ambiguous language evident in Articles 58 and 87 of UNCLOS.[11] Article 58(1) states that the high seas freedoms referred to in Article 87 of navigation and overflight apply to the EEZ including 'other internationally lawful uses of the sea related to these freedoms, such as those associated with the operation of ships, aircraft and submarine cables and pipelines'. The superficially unnecessary reference in Article 58(1) to 'the operation of ships and aircraft' was included in the convention as a euphemistic reference to military activities. Similarly the phrase *'inter alia'* ('among other things') was included in Article 87(1) as an oblique reference to extra freedoms, including the freedom to conduct military activities. The best that can be said as a consequence of this language is that there is no explicit recognition in UNCLOS of the right of third states to conduct military activities in the EEZ of a coastal state, but on the other hand there is also no express prohibition of such conduct.[12]

Some coastal states have declared security zones with restrictions on freedoms of navigation and overflight that extend into the EEZ, or have specifically claimed that other states are not authorised to conduct military exercises or manoeuvres in the EEZ without their consent. The ambiguity of the words emphasised above in Article 87 and the vagueness of interpreting whether or not something is 'compatible with the other provisions' of the Convention in UNCLOS Article 58(1) has led to considerable speculation on this issue.

While the preferred position of the United States may have been that navigational rights and freedoms by another state in a foreign EEZ are absolute, at least it would seem that 'the limitations of military uses in the exclusive economic zone are greater than those applied to similar activities carried out on the high seas'.[13] This is in line with the original views of the United States Department of State regarding the limitations on the high seas freedoms of navigation and overflight in another state's EEZ, when it noted the following:

> Intense debate arose regarding the legal nature of coastal state rights in the EEZ and their relationship to rights of other states in the zone. The consensus developed that non-resource-related high seas freedoms, including the freedoms of navigation and overflight and the freedoms to lay pipelines and submarine cables, would be preserved in the EEZ. Yet, even the exercise of these freedoms must be balanced against the exercise of EEZ rights by the coastal state.[14]

Balancing the exercise of high seas freedoms against the rights and duties of the coastal state raises the issue of 'due regard'. UNCLOS Article 56(2) provides that a coastal state should have 'due regard' to the rights and duties of other states in its EEZ, while UNCLOS Article 58(3) requires other states to have 'due regard' to the rights and duties of the coastal state in exercising *their* rights and duties in the EEZ. The vexed issue is determining the nature of the activities that do not have due regard to the rights and duties of the other party. For example, while foreign naval forces may operate in an EEZ, or pass through it, under the high seas freedoms of navigation and overflight available under UNCLOS Article 87 and extended to the EEZ under Article 58(1), they must do so with due regard to the rights and duties of the coastal state. But what type of activity by these forces would not have this due regard? An American view is that it is the duty of the flag state alone and not the right of the coastal state to enforce this *due regard* obligation,[15] but it is not that easy and there is a practical problem with interpreting what constitutes 'due regard' and what does not. Should for example, military exercises be conducted in a marine protected area legitimately established by a coastal state? Or is it appropriate for foreign warships in another state's EEZ to order away the coastal surveillance aircraft of the coastal state exercising its right to monitor activities in its EEZ?

The United States has steadfastly maintained a liberal interpretation of the rights and freedoms other states enjoy in the EEZ of a coastal state, but on the other hand, some coastal states have sought to strengthen ('thicken') the extent of their jurisdiction over their EEZ by, for example, claiming that other states should not be able to conduct certain activities such as military operations, military surveying, intelligence collection and hydrographic surveying in their EEZ without their permission. Some coastal states require that their consent be given to such activities while others, particularly the United States, argue strongly that the activities are part of the freedoms of navigation and overflight available in the EEZ through a plain reading of UNCLOS Articles 58 and 87. This situation has led a leading American exponent of the law of the sea to claim that 'Excessive EEZ claims are the major source of instability in the international law of the sea'.[16] Interpreting the rights and duties of coastal states in their EEZs vis-à-vis those of other states has become a wicked problem of maritime security in East Asia.[17]

Some regional countries have tended to 'territorialise' the EEZ in that they are looking upon the EEZ as part of their sovereign territory rather than as an area of maritime space where they have sovereign rights over resources and jurisdiction over the maritime activities specified in UNCLOS Article 56(1)(b), i.e. the establishment and use of artificial islands, installations and structures; marine scientific research; and the protection and preservation of the marine environment. As Bernard Oxman the eminent American international lawyer has observed, the EEZ has always been perceived in 'quasiterritorial' terms.[18] This was also the fear of Ken Booth when he perceptively noted over 30 years ago that:

> It may take half a century but unilateralist drives to parcel parts of the ocean will continue and will be legitimised by the territorialist mood of the international community. As this development unfolds, and as state control intensifies over larger patches of the sea, greater meaning will be invested in the new boundaries which are inevitably the

outcome of the process. Nations will feel protective and sensitive – indeed patriotic – about these patches of ocean.[19]

In trying to 'territorialise' its EEZ, a coastal state is failing to distinguish between the separate concepts of 'sovereignty' and 'sovereign rights'. This failure is 'at the core of many Law of the Sea related disputes among states'.[20] Sovereignty and sovereign rights are very different. 'Sovereignty' is what a coastal state exercises over its internal waters, territorial sea and archipelagic waters while it exercises sovereign rights over the resources of its EEZ and continental shelf. 'Sovereign rights' pertain to a functional jurisdiction, notably over resources and environmental protection that is more limited in character than 'sovereignty'. A potential problem for the region arises here in that two key regional languages, Chinese and Japanese, translate 'sovereign rights' and 'sovereignty' as the same word – *zhuquan* (主权) in Chinese and *shuken* (主権) in Japanese. This may explain some of the misunderstandings over just what a coastal state is claiming in its EEZ.

The EEZ as international waters

The United States includes the EEZ within the scope of 'international waters'. It has coined this expression to describe collectively the high seas, the EEZ and the contiguous zone. These are defined by the US Navy's, *Commander's Handbook on the Law of Naval Operations* as 'All waters seaward of the territorial sea are in international waters which the high seas freedoms of navigation and overflight are preserved to the international community'.[21] This handbook makes no mention of the limitations in UNCLOS on the high seas freedoms of navigation and overflight in an EEZ posed by the 'due regard' requirement and the need for foreign states exercising their high seas freedoms in the EEZ of another state to 'comply with the laws and regulations adopted by the coastal state in accordance with the provisions of this Convention and other rules of international law in so far as they are not incompatible with this Part'.[22]

Other authoritative sources in the United States have also chosen to make no reference to these limitations when describing freedoms of navigation in an EEZ. For example, the guide published by the Belfer Center on Freedoms of Navigation in the South China Sea states that 'The exclusive economic zone is considered part of international waters. States do not have the right to limit navigation in the exclusive economic zone'.[23] There was no reference to the 'due regard' qualification. Thus the guide set aside the carefully balanced nature of the EEZ regime in UNCLOS.

Similarly when the Congressional Research Service (CRS) in Washington produced a report on maritime territorial and EEZ disputes involving

China, it did not acknowledge important aspects of the EEZ regime.[24] It failed to acknowledge that coastal states have jurisdiction in their EEZs over marine scientific research and the protection and preservation of the marine environment. They have a right and a duty to exercise this jurisdiction, as well as their jurisdiction over economic activities. Importantly also, the CRS report did not acknowledge that under UNCLOS, states exercising their high seas freedoms in another country's EEZ should do so with 'due regard' to the rights and duties of that country. By not recognising these qualifications and repeatedly referring to the EEZ as 'international waters', the CRS report turned the clock back to the American position prior to UNCLOS when it argued that the EEZ was an extension inwards of the high seas.[25] This all looks as though now that the United States is not accepting important aspects of the EEZ regime as established by UNCLOS.

Describing the EEZ as 'international waters' is misleading. The term 'international waters' is not used in UNCLOS and it is not a legal term of art. While the EEZ is an area where high seas freedoms of navigation and overflight are preserved limited by the qualifications noted above, it is also a zone where the relevant coastal state has important rights and duties. In an example of misleading language, American commentators frequently refer to the South China Sea as 'international waters', ignoring that it is comprised almost entirely of the EEZs of the littoral countries subject to the regime of enclosed and semi-enclosed seas in UNCLOS Part IX.

As the United States is not yet a party to UNCLOS, use of the term 'international waters' can open the United States up to criticism by China and other coastal states that it does not respect the rights and duties of a foreign state in its EEZ. As a senior American practitioner of the law of the sea has observed:

> ... continued reliance on the term 'international waters' by the United States muddies the waters and unnecessarily allows China to divert attention from the legitimacy of the US position by arguing that the United States does not know the difference between the EEZ and the high seas. The United States should therefore cease to use the term 'international waters' when referring to its lawful military activities in the EEZ.[26]

Vexed issues

Military activities

It has been said that UNCLOS 'is replete with ambiguity concerning military uses of the sea'.[27] As Kaye has noted, UNCLOS 'does not deal with security issues to a significant extent' and 'almost completely avoids consideration of the laws of naval warfare'.[28] He goes on to note that the *San Remo Manual on Armed Conflicts at Sea* makes it clear that armed conflicts can take place 'in certain circumstances, in the EEZ of a neutral State', but that 'belligerents must have due regard to the uses to which another State may wish to put its EEZ, and avoid damage to the coastal State'.[29]

Practical problems arise because terms such as *military activities*, *military exercises* and *military surveying* are not particularly precise. Military activities and exercises can cover a range of naval operations from non-delaying and inoffensive passage exercises by transiting warships through various forms of surveillance and information-gathering to major exercises or operations involving ships, submarine and aircraft, possibly including the use of live fire.

The United States insists on the freedom to conduct military activities in a foreign EEZ out of concern that its naval and air access and mobility could be severely restricted by any global trend towards 'thickening jurisdiction' over the EEZ. The ability to conduct military activities in the EEZ, including military surveying and intelligence collection, is justified on the basis that they are part of the normal high seas freedoms of navigation and overflight that are available in an EEZ under UNCLOS. However, some coastal states, including Bangladesh, China, Malaysia, India, Pakistan and Thailand, contend that other states cannot carry out military exercises or manoeuvres in or over their EEZ without their consent. The concern of these states is that uninvited military activities could threaten their national security or undermine their sovereign rights over resources. For example, when Thailand ratified UNCLOS in May 2011, it made the following statement:

> The Government of the Kingdom of Thailand understands that, in the exclusive economic zone, enjoyment of the freedom of navigation in accordance with relevant provisions of the Convention excludes any non-peaceful use without the consent of the coastal State, in particular, military exercises or other activities which may affect the rights or interests of the coastal State; and it also excludes the threat or use of force against the territorial integrity, political independence, peace or security of the coastal State.[30]

This declaration is very similar to China's position on military activities in an EEZ. It is understood that Washington made strong diplomatic representations to Thailand against such a statement, but Thailand went ahead regardless. Clearly, the United States' position on these law of the sea issues is not helped by it not yet being a party to UNCLOS. It seems hypocritical of a non-party to the convention to lecture a potential party on how to interpret it.

The basic due regard principle 'requires states engaging in military activities not to unreasonably interfere with the exercise of the right of the coastal state to explore and exploit the natural resources of the EEZ'.[31] Non-interference with the coastal state's duty to preserve and protect the marine environment of the EEZ should be added to that principle. For example, scheduling an exercise in an area of intensive fishing activity declared by the coastal state, or in a marine park or marine protected area declared by the coastal state as required by article 194(5) of UNCLOS,[32] could be considered not to have due regard to the rights and duties of the coastal state. Similarly, the military activities of other states should not interfere with the legitimate surveillance and enforcement activities of the coastal state aimed at protecting its rights or preventing pollution in the EEZ. It might be regarded as inappropriate, for example, for military forces of another state to order away a *bona fide* surveillance aircraft of the coastal state from their area of operations.

Marine scientific research

Marine scientific research is the general term used to describe those activities undertaken to expand scientific knowledge of the marine environment. There is a tendency in practice to use the term 'marine scientific research' loosely when referring to all kinds of data collection (research) conducted at sea. However, not all data collection conducted at sea necessarily comes within the scope of the marine scientific research regime established by UNCLOS Part XIII that broadly requires that such research should only be conducted in an EEZ with the permission of the coastal state. Many argue that other activities, such as resource exploration, prospecting and hydrographic surveying are governed by different legal regimes. However, these activities may be difficult to distinguish in practice,[33] and this is a large part of the problem.

Another unresolved issue with the EEZ regime is interpreting what constitutes marine scientific research in the context of UNCLOS Article 56(b)(ii) that provides that the coastal state has jurisdiction over such research in its EEZ.[34] However, while the coastal state might regulate marine scientific research in its EEZ and on its continental shelf, the United States believes that hydrographic and military surveys are freedoms that the coastal state cannot regulate. It argues that they are freedoms captured by the vague expressions 'other internationally lawful uses of the sea' in UNCLOS Article 58(1) and '*inter alia*' in Article 87(1). A difficulty arises because UNCLOS does not define the key terms 'marine scientific research', 'survey activities', 'hydrographic survey' or 'military survey'. Indeed attempts at UNCLOS III to include a definition of marine scientific research in the Convention were unsuccessful.[35] The vexed issue now is whether 'hydrographic surveys' and the different types of military data collection, referred to by the United States as 'military surveys', fall within the regime of marine scientific research and thus should be within the jurisdiction of a coastal state in its EEZ.

Military surveys and hydrographic surveys

Surveying activities in an EEZ are a controversial issue, particularly with regard to whether or not they are a form of marine scientific research under the jurisdiction of the coastal state in its EEZ. The United States equates the right to conduct what it calls 'military surveys' in an EEZ without prior notification to, or the permission of the coastal state with a similar right to conduct hydrographic surveys in an EEZ. Other maritime powers hold a similar position although their terminology may be different.

Military surveys are activities undertaken in ocean and coastal waters involving marine data collection (whether or not classified) for military purposes. Such data is important, even essential, for effective submarine operations, anti-submarine warfare, mine warfare and mine countermeasures, particularly in waters such as the South and East China Seas where oceanographic and underwater acoustic conditions vary widely with uneven bottom topography, fast tidal streams and a relatively high level of marine life. While the means of data collection used in military surveys may sometimes be the same as that used in marine scientific research, information from such activities, regardless of security classification, is intended not for use by the general scientific community, but by the military.[36] The United States reserves the right to conduct these surveys outside foreign territorial seas and archipelagic waters, and that to 'provide prior notice or request permission would create an adverse precedent for restrictions on mobility and flexibility of military survey operation'.[37]

While UNCLOS has established a clear regime for marine scientific research, there is no specific provision in UNCLOS for hydrographic surveying. Some coastal states require consent with respect to hydrographic surveys conducted in their EEZ by other states while it is the opinion of the United States and other maritime powers that hydrographic surveys can be conducted freely in the EEZ. This latter position is based on the notion that hydrographic surveys are conducted to enhance the safety of navigation and are therefore a freedom as an internationally lawful use of the sea associated with the operations of ships in accordance with UNCLOS Article 58(1).[38]

The maritime powers in arguing that 'survey activities' are not marine scientific research point out that UNCLOS distinguishes between 'research' and 'marine scientific research' on the one hand, and 'hydrographic surveys' and 'survey activities' on the other, because these are sometimes referred to separately in the Convention. However, this is a questionable argument as it can also be argued that the use of separate terms provides a 'catch-all' phrase for the types of research activities that are either prohibited or require the authorisation of the coastal state in particular circumstances.[39]

It is significant that all the separate references to surveying activities are in the context of the passage regimes in UNCLOS rather than with regard to rights and duties in an EEZ. Article 19(2)(j) states that ships exercising the right of innocent passage should not carry out any 'research or survey' activities. Article 40 states that during transit passage of straits used for international navigation 'foreign ships, including marine scientific research and hydrographic survey ships, may not carry out any research or survey activities without the prior authorization of the States bordering straits'. Article 40 applies *mutatis mutandis* to archipelagic sea lanes passage in accordance with UNCLOS Article 54. The separate terms 'research' and 'survey' are used in these articles to make sure that these associated activities are both prohibited during passage rather than to establish a separate regime for surveying. They were included for precisely the opposite reason to what is now argued – that is to make clear that it could not be argued that a 'survey' was different to 'research' and thus permissible in an EEZ.

This position is supported by the history of how these separate words came to be included in UNCLOS.[40] A proposal by Fiji at the second session of UNCLOS III in 1974 became the origin of the final language of Article 40 after an earlier proposal by Fiji at the Sea-Bed Committee provided that foreign warships exercising the right of innocent passage through the territorial sea should not 'undertake any hydrographical survey work or any marine research activities'.[41] This was out of concern that all forms of research activity by transiting ships were prohibited rather than to establish separate regimes for research and surveys.

The technology of hydrographic surveys and the utility of hydrographic data have changed considerably since UNCLOS was negotiated. Accurate surveys can now be conducted using differential global positioning systems (DGPS) without the need for shore stations and can also be conducted by aircraft. Apart from navigational safety, the uses of hydrographic data extend to planning the exploration and exploitation of marine resources, determining seaward limits of national jurisdiction, facilitating coastal zone management, and developing new ports and harbours. It is pedantic to argue that hydrographic surveys are only required for navigational safety and thus a freedom of navigation.

Hydrographic knowledge of adjacent waters is now an essential element of national infrastructure and development,[42] and it is very hard these days to identify any hydrographic data, including that collected by military surveying ships, which would not have potential value to the coastal state.[43] Bathymetric charts providing a description of seabed topography are a routine output of hydrographic surveys and a basic tool of resource exploitation. Hydrographic data in the EEZ has economic value to the coastal state and the coastal state should be in a position to manage and control such data, regardless of how and by whom it was collected. This data is subject to copyright and no longer may navigational and hydrographic information on nautical charts issued by one country be freely copied by another state on to its own nautical charts.

This position is reflected in the definition of a hydrographic survey in the International Hydrographic Dictionary published by the International Hydrographic Organization (IHO):

> A survey having for its principal purpose the determination of data relating to bodies of water. A hydrographic survey may consist of the determination of one or several of the following classes of data: depth of water, configuration and nature of the bottom; directions and force of currents; heights and times of tide and water stages; and location of topographic features and fixed objects for survey and navigation purposes.

This definition does not relate hydrographic surveying specifically to navigational purpose. The focus of the definition is on the nature of the data collected rather on the purpose of the data collection. It is anachronistic now to argue that hydrographic surveys are not part of marine scientific research and related only to navigational safety.

The United States equates 'military surveys' with 'hydrographic surveys', but this gives rise to problems. The United Kingdom similarly believes that what it calls 'military data gathering' may be conducted in an EEZ without prior notice to, or permission from the coastal state. The term 'military data gathering' may be preferable because it associates the activity with the general right to conduct military activities in the EEZ of another state rather than with the questionable right to conduct hydrographic surveys in the EEZ without coastal state notice or consent. The argument that data collection purely for military purposes is a freedom of navigation available in an EEZ has more strength than the argument that hydrographic surveys can be conducted in an EEZ without the consent of the coastal state.

Surveillance and intelligence collection

A debate has arisen over the issue of military and intelligence-gathering activities in an EEZ. Again as with 'military surveys', the United States and others argue that these activities are captured by the phrase 'other internationally lawful uses of the sea' in UNCLOS Article 58(1) and are part of the high seas freedoms of navigation and overflight available in another country's EEZ. However, China and some regional countries argue that these activities are prejudicial to their national security and not a peaceful use of the EEZ.

It is not surprising that incidents have already occurred in the Asia-Pacific region, involving surveillance and intelligence collection activities. A Chinese fighter aircraft crashed after colliding with an American intelligence collection aircraft in China's EEZ off Hainan in April 2001, and alleged 'spy ships' have been pursued out of Japan's EEZ with one vessel even being sunk after hot pursuit into China's EEZ. In March 2009 the American ocean surveillance vessel USNS *Impeccable* was harassed by Chinese vessels in an area south of Hainan. Shortly before the *Impeccable* incident, a sister-ship, USNS *Victorious*, had earlier experienced harassment by a Chinese patrol vessel and maritime surveillance aircraft in the Yellow Sea.

In July 2017, a Chinese Navy electronic intelligence-gathering vessel was spotted in Australia's EEZ off the Queensland coast in the vicinity of Exercise Talisman Sabre, which it was almost certainly monitoring.[44] Earlier that month a similar vessel was deployed in the American EEZ off Alaska, probably gathering signals from a test of the American THAAD ballistic missile defence system. These vessels regularly track US Navy movements and at-sea exercises across the Indo-Pacific, including at RIMPAC exercises.[45] These incidents suggest hypocrisy by China in that it objects to foreign military surveillance and intelligence collection in its own EEZ while carrying out similar operations itself in the EEZs of foreign countries.

Based on current and planned naval and defence acquisitions in the Asia-Pacific region, particularly the growth of regional submarine fleets, surveillance and intelligence-gathering activities in EEZs will likely increase in the future. These activities might also become more controversial and more dangerous in the region. This trend reflects the increasing demands for technical intelligence; rapidly expanding weapon and sensor acquisition programmes, including electronic warfare capabilities; and widespread moves to develop information warfare capabilities. These activities may also be difficult to distinguish from what might be regarded as an acceptable activity in an EEZ, although the external appearance of the vessel (e.g. the aerials on a signals or electronic intelligence vessel), the equipment it is operating (e.g. the type of sonar), and its movements (e.g. whether it is manoeuvring, stopping or continually underway) might give a good lead on the nature of its data collection.

The technology of surveillance and intelligence collection has developed considerably since UNCLOS was agreed. A particular debate has emerged over the use of active signals intelligence activities that may be conducted by ships or aircraft and can be deliberately provocative to generate programmed responses.[46] This is sometimes referred to as 'tickling' to disrupt the coastal state's communications systems, or to provoke a response from its missile or radar systems thereby providing information about missile control frequencies, for example.[47]

Regional issues

The EEZ regime has great strategic significance, particularly in the Western Pacific and East Asia where large areas of ocean and sea are enclosed as EEZs (see Figure 3.1). The introduction of the EEZ regime has had far-reaching implications in East Asia. Regional seas are mainly enclosed as the EEZ of one coastal state or another and the delimitation of EEZ boundaries has proven difficult. Relatively few EEZ boundaries have been agreed so far in the region.[48] Rather more continental shelf boundaries have been agreed. These large areas of maritime jurisdiction under the EEZ regime have provided strategic justification for building up a country's maritime security forces to enforce jurisdiction and protect sovereign rights in this broad zone. The lack of EEZ boundaries increases the risks of incidents between the security forces of adjacent countries.

Incidents and disputes have occurred in the region related to the conduct of research and surveys in the EEZ. In March 2001, India lodged protests with the United States and United Kingdom over violations of its EEZ by military survey ships. The ships involved were the USNS *Bowditch* and HMS *Scott*. The *Bowditch* was detected 30 nautical miles from Nicobar Island and was reportedly carrying out 'oceanographic survey operations'.[49] After having been sighted 190 nautical miles off Diu and later near Porbandar in the Arabian Sea, the *Scott* indicated it was carrying out military surveys but declined to provide any further information.[50]

These types of incident could well have escalated.[51] Other major incidents include the surveillance and intelligence collection incidents already mentioned. In the case of the *Impeccable* incident in March 2009, the United States argued strongly that the operations of the *Impeccable* were a legitimate freedom of navigation available to other states in a country's EEZ.[52] The incident became a catalyst for direct

68 *Exclusive economic zone issues*

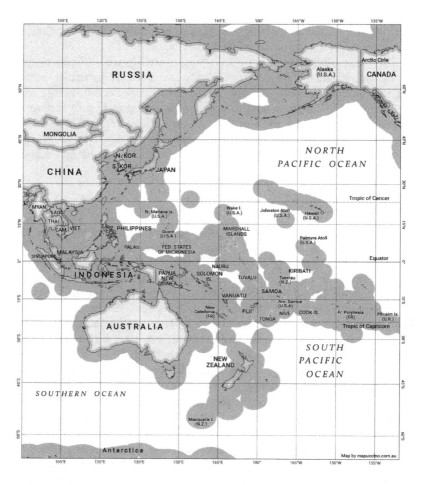

Figure 3.1 EEZs in the Western and Central Pacific.

American intervention in affairs of the South China Sea. The Chinese view was that the United States was trying to interpret UNCLOS in its own interests and that the operations of the *Impeccable* were contrary to its peace, good order or security and that they also constituted marine scientific research that required its consent.[53] The *Impeccable* was likely conducting research related to the ability to track Chinese submarines moving out of their base on Hainan but this probably was not marine scientific research.

This *Impeccable* incident became one 'trigger' for United States–China tensions because it increased Chinese sensitivity to American operations in the South China Sea and alarmed Washington. On the American side, it demonstrated a possible Chinese threat to the freedoms of navigation and overflight. American interest in these freedoms in the South China Sea is mainly associated with military ships and aircraft and their freedom to conduct certain military research and survey activities in a foreign EEZ. However, there seems little doubt about their availability of freedoms of navigation to commercial shipping in the South China Sea. China has stated on several occasions that it respects general freedoms of navigation and overflight in the South China Sea. These are also respected in Article 3 of the 2002 Declaration on the Conduct of Parties in the South China Sea (DOC) signed by China.[54]

Law of the sea issues are a fundamental area of disagreement between China and the United States. China has significant claims under the law of the sea judged by Washington to be excessive.[55] On the other hand, and as was argued earlier, the United States appears not to accept some aspects of the EEZ regime as established by UNCLOS.

Way forward

The most intractable problems with freedoms of navigation in the Asia-Pacific region arise from the ambiguities and grey areas in UNCLOS regarding the EEZ regime. For all these reasons, the EEZ remains 'a zone of tension between coastal state control and maritime state use of the sea'.[56] As technology changes, the requirements of maritime governance are more appreciated and levels of activity by regional maritime security forces increase, the frequency and intensity of disputes over rights and duties in the EEZ may increase in the region. There are several ways forward out of the current impasse.[57] The first is some sort of bilateral agreement on the issues between Beijing and Washington, similar to the agreement that the United States and the Soviet Union reached on innocent passage, but that seems unlikely. The current Military Maritime Consultative Agreement (MMCA) has been singularly unsuccessful at addressing relevant questions,[58] and even if China conceded any ground on the issue, other regional countries of like views may not fall in behind China.

The second possibility is that of international arbitration, but that is also unlikely. Neither of the two major powers would be attracted to this and, in any case, it is not currently available while the United States is not a party to UNCLOS. Then even if the United States became a party to the convention, it could well decline application of mandatory dispute resolution procedures to the case because it involves military activities.

UNCLOS Part XV establishes a regime for the settlement of disputes between parties to the Convention concerning the interpretation or application of the principles of UNCLOS. Article 298 establishes optional exceptions to the application of the compulsory procedure in Part XV.[59] These include disputes concerning 'military activities, including military activities by government vessels and aircraft engaged in non-commercial service'.

The third possibility is some regional guidelines that, even if non-binding, would at least provide some guidance on the nature of activities which could be considered as not having due regard to the rights and duties of the other party. With this objective in mind, the Ship and Ocean Foundation of Japan – now the Ocean Policy Research Foundation (OPRF) developed the *Guidelines for Navigation and Overflight in the Exclusive Economic Zone* issued in 2005.[60] These set out broad principles of common understanding regarding certain aspects of navigation and over flight in an EEZ, including military and intelligence gathering activities. They were framed in exhortatory rather than obligatory language and reflected the need for better understanding of the rights and obligations of States operating in the EEZ of another country. However, these guidelines were not considered by any regional forum, and an American expert on the law of the sea rejected them as 'unacceptable even as a starting point'.[61]

In view of the lack of acceptance of the Guidelines, the OPRF issued a revised simpler document in 2014, *Principles for Building Confidence and Security in the Exclusive Economic Zones of the Asia-Pacific*,[62] with the aim of overcoming the objections to the earlier guidelines. The *Principles* focus on the central issues of misunderstanding and ambiguity with regard to rights and duties in the EEZ: the interpretation of the term 'due regard', the lack of a universal definition of 'marine scientific research' and the scope of activities in the EEZ contrary to the norm that the EEZ should be reserved for peaceful purposes.

The *Principles* accept that military activities in an EEZ are legitimate, subject to having due regard to the rights of the coastal state. The basic principle is that military activities conducted lawfully by another state in and above the EEZ of a coastal state should not interfere with or endanger the rights and jurisdiction of the coastal state to protect and manage its resources and environment; or involve marine scientific research. The *Principles* identify examples of areas where other states should avoid conducting military activities, such as in areas rich in living or non-living resources; areas of active resource exploration and exploitation; marine parks or marine protected areas declared by the coastal state in accordance with internationally accepted standards; areas subject to ships' routeing and traffic separation schemes adopted in accordance with internationally accepted standards; or near submarine cables and pipelines on the seabed of the EEZ clearly marked by the coastal state on large-scale charts.[63] They provide that 'Hydrographic surveying in the EEZ requires consent of the coastal State when the data collected affect the exclusive rights and jurisdiction of the coastal State'.[64]

The *Principles* have not to date been considered by any regional Track One forum.[65] It would be a significant confidence-building measure if they were to achieve some form of regional acceptance. Unfortunately, Track One forums tend to steer clear of wicked problems such as attempting to reach some agreement on the freedoms of navigation in an EEZ. For example, the ASEAN Regional Forum (ARF) Inter-Sessional Meeting on Maritime Security has convened Workshops on Enacting UNCLOS and other International Instruments to address emerging maritime issues but these have limited their discussions to bland issues such as IUU fishing, information-sharing and the problem of plastics in the oceans.

Lastly, the United States is not acting judiciously on matters of the EEZ and freedoms of navigation within that zone. It is both part of the cause of problems with the EEZ and part of their solutions. While not a party to UNCLOS, it is not backward in preaching its interpretation of key provisions of the convention to regional countries. However, it also appears to ignore important features of the EEZ regime, the *sui generis* nature of which is so important to regional countries. It also fails to support Part IX of UNCLOS, and the exhortations therein to the littoral countries of the South China Sea to cooperate in managing the sea and certain activities within it.

American commentators continue to talk about the South China Sea as 'international waters' or as part of the 'global commons' or the 'maritime commons'. They are not. Rather they are parts of the EEZs of one or another of the bordering countries, which have significant rights and duties in such waters that need to be respected. States exercising their high seas freedoms of navigation in anther state's EEZ need to do so with due regard to the rights and duties of that state. It would be a good step forward for regional stability and good order in regional seas if the United States acknowledged more fully the *sui generis* nature of the EEZ and stopped referring to the semi-enclosed seas of the region as 'international waters' or as part of the 'maritime commons'.

Notes

1 UNCLOS Article 57.
2 UNCLOS Article 56(1)(b).
3 A surprising feature of the ruling in 2016 from the Arbitral Tribunal that addressed the dispute between China and the Philippines in the South China Sea was the judgment that there are no 'fully entitled' islands in the Spratly

72 Exclusive economic zone issues

group entitled to an EEZ and continental shelf. That particular ruling has implications for other EEZ claims around the world based on features that by the standard of this judgment would not qualify as 'islands'. Sam Bateman, 'The South China Sea Arbitration: Challenges and Opportunities', *The Strategist*, 2 August 2016, www.aspistrategist.org.au/south-china-sea-arbitration-challenges-opportunities/.

4 Donald R. Rothwell and Tim Stephens, *The International Law of the Sea*, Oxford: Hart Publishing Ltd, 2010, pp. 82–83.
5 Ibid., p. 83.
6 UNCLOS Article 55 states that the EEZ is subject to the specific legal regime established in UNCLOS Part V, under which the rights and jurisdiction of the coastal state and the rights and freedoms of other states are governed by the relevant provisions of the Convention.
7 George R. Galdorisi and Kevin R. Vienna, *Beyond the Law of the Sea – New Directions for US Oceans Policy*, Westport: Praeger, 1997, p. 151.
8 Stephen Rose, 'Naval Activity in the Exclusive Economic Zone – Troubled Waters Ahead?', *Ocean Development and International Law*, Vol. 21, No. 2, 1990, p. 127.
9 R.R. Churchill and A.V. Lowe, *The Law of the Sea*, 3rd edn, Manchester: Manchester University Press, 1999, p. 427.
10 James Kraska, *Maritime Power and the Law of the Sea*, New York: Oxford University Press, 2011, p. 239.
11 Captain G.V. Galdorisi, USN (ret) and Commander A.G. Kaufman, JAGC, USN, 'Military Activities in the Exclusive Economic Zone: Preventing Uncertainty and Defusing Conflict', *Californian Western International Law Journal*, Vol. 32, 2001–2002, p. 271.
12 Natalie Klein, *Maritime Security and the Law of the Sea*, Oxford: Oxford University Press, 2012, p. 219.
13 F.O. Vicuna, *The Exclusive Economic Zone: Regime and Legal Nature Under International Law*, Cambridge: Cambridge University Press, 1989, p. 111.
14 US State Department's report *Limits in the Seas No. 112* on excessive maritime claims, www.state.gov/documents/organization/58381.pdf.
15 Galdorisi and Vienna, *Beyond the Law of the Sea*, p. 151.
16 Kraska, *Maritime Power and the Law of the Sea*, p. 13.
17 Sam Bateman, 'Solving the "Wicked Problems" of Maritime Security – Are Regional Forums up to the Task?', *Contemporary Southeast Asia*, Vol. 33, No. 1, 2011, pp. 7–10.
18 Bernard Oxman, 'The Territorial Temptation: A Siren Song at Sea,' *American Journal of International Law*, 100, October 2006, p. 839.
19 Ken Booth, *Law, Force and Diplomacy at Sea*, London: Allen and Unwin, 1985, pp. 44–45.
20 CSCAP Memorandum No. 6, *The Practice of the Law of the Sea in the Asia Pacific*, December 2002, p. 4.
21 US Navy, *The Commander's Handbook on the Law of Naval Operations*, NWP 1-14M/MCTP 11-10B/COMDTPUB P5800.7A, Edition August 2017, paragraph 1–6, www.nwc.navy.mil/ILD/Commander's%Handbook.htm.
22 UNCLOS Article 58(3).
23 Eleanor Freund, *Freedom of Navigation in the South China Sea: A Practical Guide*, Belfer Center for Science and International Affairs, Harvard Kennedy School, June 2017, p. 15, www.belfercenter.org/publication/freedom-navigation-south-china-sea-practical-guide.

24 Ronald O'Rourke, *Maritime Territorial and Exclusive Economic Zone (EEZ) Disputes Involving China: Issues for Congress* CRS Report No. R42784, 18 September 2015, https://fas.org/sgp/crs/row/R42784.pdf.
25 Sam Bateman, 'Turning Back the Clock on UNCLOS', *The Strategist*, 20 August 2015, www.aspistrategist.org.au/turning-back-the-clock-on-unclos/.
26 Raul (Pete) Pedrozo, 'Preserving Navigational Rights and Freedoms: The Right to Conduct Military Activities in China's Exclusive Economic Zone', *Chinese Journal of International Law*, Vol. 9, No. 1, March 2010, p. 19.
27 Dale G. Stephens, 'The Impact of the 1982 Law of the Sea Convention on the Conduct of Peacetime Naval/Military Operations', *Californian Western International Law Journal*, Vol. 29, 1998–1999, p. 283.
28 Stuart Kaye, 'Freedom of Navigation in a Post 9/11 World: Security and Creeping Jurisdiction', in David Freestone, Richard Barnes and David Ong (eds), *The Law of the Sea: Progress and Prospects*, Oxford: Oxford University Press, 2006, pp. 347–364.
29 Ibid. p. 353.
30 United Nations, Statement by Thailand on Ratifying UNCLOS, 25 May 2011, C.N.291.2011.TREATIES-4 (Depositary Notification), http://treaties.un.org/doc/Publication/CN/2011/CN.291.2011-Eng.pdf.
31 Robert Beckman, 'Military Activities in the Exclusive Economic Zone: Towards a Common Understanding' in Yang Razali Kassim (ed.), *Strategic Currents*, Singapore: Institute of Defence and Strategic Studies, Nanyang Technological University, 2006, p. 42.
32 This article requires the coastal state to take the measures necessary to protect and preserve rare or fragile ecosystems as well as the habitat of depleted, threatened or endangered species and other forms of marine life.
33 Sam Bateman, 'Hydrographic Surveying in the EEZ: Differences and Overlaps with Marine Scientific Research', *Marine Policy*, Vol. 29, 2005, pp. 166–169.
34 This section is based on Sam Bateman, 'A Response to Pedrozo – The Wider Utility of Hydrographic Surveys', *Chinese Journal of International Law*, 2011; doi: 10.1093/chinesejil/jmq036; and an earlier paper: Sam Bateman, 'Hydrographic Surveying in Exclusive Economic Zones – Is It Marine Scientific Research?' in Myron H. Nordquist, Tommy T.B. Koh and John Norton Moore (eds), *Freedom of Seas, Passage Rights and the 1982 Law of the Sea Convention*, Dordrecht: Martinus Nijhoff Publishers, 2009, pp. 105–131.
35 Alfred H.A. Soons, *Implementation of the Marine Scientific Research Regime in the South Pacific – Final Report*, FFA Report 95/14 and SOPAC Joint Contribution Report 101, Forum Fisheries Agency, Honiara, 24 October 1994, p. 6.
36 J. Ashley Roach and Robert W. Smith, 'Excessive Maritime Claims', *International Law Studies No. 66*, Naval War College, Newport R.I., 1994, p. 248.
37 Ibid. p. 249.
38 Kraska, *Maritime Power and the Law of the Sea*, p. 275.
39 Sam Bateman, 'A Response to Pedrozo', paras 7–8.
40 Verbal advice in Honolulu on 10 December 2003 from Judge Alexander Yankov then member of the International Tribunal on the Law of the Sea and formerly Chairman of the Third Committee of UNCLOS III (1973–1982) that addressed marine scientific research issues.
41 Satya N. Nandan and Shabtai N. Rosenne (eds), *United Nations Convention on the Law of the Sea 1982 – A Commentary*, Dordrecht: Martinus Nijhoff, 1993, pp. 350–351.

74 *Exclusive economic zone issues*

42 As discussed in Chapter 1 – The Need for a Hydrographic Service in IHO publication *M-2 – National Maritime Policies and Hydrographic Services*, International Hydrographic Bureau, Monaco, 2001 (available at www.iho.shom.fr/PUBLICATIONS/download.htm).
43 These arguments are developed more fully in Sam Bateman, 'Hydrographic Surveying in Exclusive Economic Zones: Jurisdictional Issues', *International Hydrographic Review (New Series)*, Vol. 5, No. 1, 2004, pp. 24–33.
44 Euan Graham, 'China's Naval Surveillance off Australia: Good News and Bad', *The Interpreter*, 24 July 2017, www.lowyinstitute.org/the-interpreter/china-s-naval-surveillance-australia-good-news-and-bad.
45 Choi Chi-yuk, 'China Sends Spy Ship to Monitor US-led RIMPAC War Games off Hawaii', *South China Morning Post*, 14 July 2018, www.scmp.com/news/china/diplomacy-defence/article/2155289/china-sends-spy-ship-monitor-us-led-rimpac-war-games.
46 Klein, *Maritime Security*, p. 218.
47 Mark J. Valencia, 'A 'New Normal' in the South China Sea?', *East Asia Forum*, 26 May 2018, www.eastasiaforum.org/2018/05/26/a-new-normal-in-the-south-china-sea/.
48 The situation in 1998 with maritime boundaries in East Asia is described in Sam Bateman, 'Economic Growth, Marine Resources and Naval Arms in East Asia – A Deadly Triangle?', *Marine Policy*, Vol. 22, No. 4–5, 1998, pp. 297–306. The situation has only changed since then by agreements over boundaries between Indonesia and Vietnam (a continental shelf boundary only) and Vietnam and China in the Gulf of Tonkin.
49 Galdorisi and Kaufman, 'Military Activities in the Exclusive Economic Zone', p. 294.
50 Ibid., pp. 294–295.
51 Mark J. Valencia, 'Foreign Military Activities in Asian EEZs Conflict Ahead', *NBR Special Report No. 27*, 13 May 2011, pp. 9–11, www.nbr.org/publication/foreign-military-activities-in-asian-eezs-conflict-ahead/.
52 Strong defences of the American position might be found in Jonathan G. Odom, 'The True "Lies" of the *Impeccable* Incident: What Really Happened, Who Disregarded International Law, and Why Every Nation (Outside of China) Should Be Concerned', *Michigan State Journal of International Law*, Vol. 18, No. 3, pp. 1–42; and Pedrozo, 'Preserving Navigational Rights and Freedoms'.
53 The Chinese position is described in: Zhang Haiwen, 'Is It Safeguarding the Freedom of Navigation or Maritime Hegemony of the United States? – Comments on Raul (Pete) Pedrozo's Article on Military Activities in the EEZ', *Chinese Journal of International Law*, Vol. 9, No. 1, March, 2010, pp. 31–48.
54 2002 Declaration on the Conduct of Parties in the South China Sea (DOC), https://cil.nus.edu.sg/wp-content/uploads/2017/07/2002-Declaration-on-the-Conduct-of-Parties-in-the-South-China-Sea.pdf.
55 See, for example, US Department of State, Bureau of Oceans and International Environmental Scientific Affairs, *Limits in the Seas No. 117 – Straight Baseline Claim – China*, 9 July 1996.
56 Galdorisi and Vienna, *Beyond the Law of the Sea*, 1997, p. 257.
57 Valencia, 'Foreign Military Activities in Asian EEZs', pp. 15–18.
58 Ibid., p. 16.
59 UNCLOS Article 298(1)(b).

60 The Guidelines are available at: www.sof.or.jp/topics/2005_e/pdf/20051205_e. pdf. A discussion of the Guidelines may be found in Sam Bateman, 'Prospective Guidelines for Navigation and Overflight in the Exclusive Economic Zone', *Maritime Studies*, No. 144, September/October 2005, pp. 17–28.
61 Pedrozo, 'Preserving Navigational Rights and Freedoms', p. 28.
62 Available at www.spf.org/_opri_media/publication/pdf/2014_03_02.pdf.
63 Principle V(4).
64 Principle VII(4).
65 Track One forums are where ministers and senior officials meet to discuss major issues of mutual interest. Track Two forums are non-official meetings where academics, business people and non-government organisations, as well as officials acting in their private capacity, meet to discuss issues of common interest. Track 1.5 forums denote a situation in which official and non-official actors work together to resolve problems.

4 Building understandings and confidence

Different perspectives

The many legal complexities with the law of the sea in the Asia-Pacific region are compounded by strategic and political factors that lead in turn to different perspectives of the freedoms of navigation. The legal factors are not necessarily paramount and may frequently be distorted or even over-ruled by other considerations. If a country wishes to pursue a particular position, then it will seek to 'bend' the law to justify its position. Many examples of this approach exist in the region for example, with the use of straight territorial sea baselines, and claims to offshore features and controls over activities in its adjacent waters that other countries might regard as illegitimate or excessive. Australia's introduction of compulsory pilotage in the Torres Strait is a notable example of how a range of political, operational and legal considerations were blended together to produce a policy outcome that was beyond what previously had been regarded as the law.[1]

When a coastal state has determined its particular approach to a maritime issue for political and strategic reasons, its international lawyers might then have to be creative in finding justification for that approach. In effect there is a political 'horse' pulling the legal 'cart', although international lawyers may well say that this is putting the 'cart before the horse'! But this is the nature of international law and, if sufficient countries adopt a particular approach, the *excessive* claim of today may well become the *customary* law of tomorrow. This would be in line with the provision in Article 31 (3) of the Vienna Convention on the Law of Treaties that in interpreting a treaty, account shall be taken of 'any subsequent practice in the application of the treaty that establishes the agreement of the parties regarding its implementation'. As Churchill notes, 'In extreme cases practice could lead to a new rule of customary international law modifying the LOS Convention'.[2]

Conflicting maritime strategies

At the heart of the different perspectives of freedoms of navigation in the Asia-Pacific region are the conflicting maritime strategies of the major Western maritime powers, particularly the United States, on the one hand, and regional countries on the other. The Western powers seek maximum freedoms of navigation while regional countries try to restrict these freedoms within their littoral waters. With their conflicting strategies, the major powers are concerned for power projection and what maritime strategists speak of as *sea control*, the ability to assert domination of maritime space for one's own purposes, albeit in a limited area for a limited period of time, while regional navies largely focus on what is termed *sea denial*, the ability to deny an adversary the use of the sea without necessarily asserting one's own use.[3]

These contrasting approaches have been highlighted in recent decades by the concern of the US Navy, in particular, for littoral operations rather than for operations on the high seas. This is evident on the United States' Joint Concept for Access and Maneuver in the Global Commons (JAM-GC) aimed at the development by some countries, particularly by China, of capabilities, such as naval mines, anti-surface missile systems ashore and afloat, and submarines, aimed at denying access to their littoral waters by an opponent's forces.[4] These sea denial strategies relate in turn to the desire of China and some other regional countries to restrict foreign military operations in their EEZs.

These contrasting strategies are also reflected in the force structure preferences of the different navies. The major Western powers focus on aircraft carriers and large amphibious ships while smaller navies in the Asia-Pacific region focus on smaller missile firing surface combatants and submarines relevant to sea denial operations in their adjacent waters. To some extent these different preferences also reflect the realities of both the more limited naval budgets of the regional countries and geography with the regional countries focused on defending their own 'backyards' rather than projecting power.

The so-called regional 'middle powers', Australia, Japan and South Korea, fall somewhere in between the strategies of the major powers and other regional countries. They aspire to large amphibious ships and even aircraft carriers but also show a strong interest in sea denial capabilities. They are also more ambivalent towards freedoms of navigation. They express a strong interest in these freedoms while also showing a tendency to restrict these freedoms in their own waters: Japan has over the years taken aggressive action against the so-called North Korean 'spy ships' in its EEZ despite these vessels theoretically having high seas freedoms of navigation;[5] South Korea has sought to restrict navigation through the Cheju Strait despite this strait being categorised as a strait used for international navigation;[6] and Australia has introduced a number of policies that other countries regard as unacceptable restrictions on freedoms of navigation, including compulsory pilotage in the Torres Strait.[7]

There is also a broader strategic context to be recognised with the struggle for hegemony in the waters of East Asia between China and the United States. As Kraska has noted 'The political disputes over freedom of navigation arise within this strategic context', referring to how the strategic competition between these major powers influences their positions on the freedoms of navigation.[8] As was noted in earlier chapters of this book, China and the United States are at odds over a range of freedom of navigation issues with China seeking to deny particular freedoms while the United States wants to assert them. With increasing strategic competition between these leading players in the region, incidents involving their different perspectives of freedoms of navigation may become more frequent unless they can achieve some common understandings, or at least agree on measures that might mitigate the risks of these incidents.

Maritime confidence-building measures

Confidence-building measures (CBMs) and preventive diplomacy are widely discussed in security discourse. CBMs can be military measures or broader initiatives encompassing almost anything that builds confidence, promotes dialogue between countries and reduces the risks of tensions and conflict. They include formal and informal measures, whether unilateral, bilateral or multilateral, which contribute to a reduction in misperception and uncertainty. The concept of confidence-building has been around for a long time. Back in 1982, the UN Comprehensive Study on Confidence-Building Measures stated that:

> the goal of confidence-building measures is to contribute to, reduce or, in some instances, even eliminate the causes for mistrust, fear, tensions and hostilities, all of which are significant factors in the continuation of the international arms build-up in various regions and, ultimately, also on a world-wide scale.[9]

The maritime domain is a fertile field for confidence-building.[10] Maritime confidence-building measures (MCBMs) might include greater clarity and understanding in the region of particular law of the sea issues.[11] These could include navigational regimes and the rights and obligations of coastal states in offshore zones. The development of agreement on a common understanding of a particular regime might constitute a significant MCBM that would both reduce the risks of conflict and enhance the governance of regional oceans and seas. Disputes over freedoms of navigation are causes of distrust and tensions and are potentially open to MCBMs.

UNCLOS is a significant MCBM in its own right. Many provisions of UNCLOS have confidence-building effects. For example, the innocent passage regime in Section 3 of the Convention places specific restrictions on warships exercising the right of innocent passage, including that submarines should transit on the surface in a foreign territorial sea. However, there are still many 'grey areas' with the law of the sea which require negotiation between interested parties. As was once observed in a reference to UNCLOS, 'the roots of disputes or conflicts are the different national views and interpretations of the same clauses and phrases written in the Convention which gives states the rights they hold dear'.[12] This is particularly so with provisions relating to the EEZ regime.

Differences on navigational issues can become dangerous when tensions exist.[13] Any measures at all that would have the effect of limiting the scope for disputation would be advantageous. Jin-Hyun Paik has observed referring to the Asia-Pacific region that the need for 'a commonly accepted interpretation is more acute in this part of the world than in any other region, mainly because the practice of the major aspects of ocean use diverges substantially among the coastal states of the region'.[14]

Some dialogue towards a common regional understanding of areas where uncertainty exists could be a worthwhile MCBM. The precedent for this activity would be the agreement between the United States and the Soviet Union on a common interpretation of the regime of innocent passage. This provides *inter alia* that neither prior notification nor authorisation is required for the innocent passage of warships, regardless of cargo, armament or means of propulsion. However, there is also concern that some MCBMs could constitute a form of 'creeping' and 'thickening' jurisdiction that would have the overall effect of increasing coastal state control over adjacent waters beyond that allowed under international law. The United States, in particular, believes that many MCBMs could be a 'slippery slope' leading to tighter restrictions on naval operations. While it is so easy to identify and talk about MCBMs, it is much harder to translate them into a plan for action.

With the numerous sovereignty disputes in East Asia, and the build-up of regional navies, maritime confidence-building has attracted attention in regional forums over the years. Back in August 1995, for example, the Second Meeting of the ASEAN Regional Forum (ARF) in Brunei identified a range of measures related to maritime confidence-building.[15] But the only ones of these fully implemented are those of cooperative humanitarian assistance and disaster relief, and the introduction of a multilateral agreement to prevent incidents at sea. The last step was achieved through agreement in 2014 by the Western Pacific Naval Symposium (WPNS) to the Code for Unplanned Encounters between Ships (CUES).

INCSEA agreements

Measures to prevent or manage incidents between the maritime security forces of different countries, or incident at sea (INCSEA) agreements, whether bilateral or multilateral, are classic MCBMs. Several INCSEA agreements already exist in the region. The one between the United States and Russia, originally agreed in 1972 between the Soviet Union and the United States, is a key example of a practical MCBM. In the region, Russia has also signed INCSEA agreements with Japan and South Korea. However, these INCSEA agreements are not necessarily good models for the region. First, they relate to the activities of navies that routinely conducted close surveillance of each other's exercises and operations. Second, the agreements are limited to high seas activities and not to EEZs or territorial seas. Any attempt to develop an agreement to apply in EEZs would open up the controversial question of the nature of the military activities that another state may conduct in the EEZ of a coastal state. Third, their success can be attributed partly to the fact that they are all bilateral. The more interests around the table, the harder it is to negotiate an agreement. Lastly, submerged submarine operations are excluded from these agreements.

The United States and China have agreed a set of bilateral agreements: the 2014 Memorandum of Understanding (MOU) on Notification of Major Military Activities Confidence-Building Measures Mechanism (MOU-CBMM); and the 2014 MOU on the Rules of Behaviour for the Safety of Air and Maritime Encounters (MOU-Rules) and its set of annexes dealing with the safety of Air and Maritime Encounters. The annex dealing with surface-to-surface encounters was agreed at the same time as the major agreements but the one on air-to-air encounters not until a year later.[16] This air-to-air annex has been criticised as unhelpful because it adds a new layer of nonbinding provisions that merely create unhelpful ambiguity and dilute China's pre-existing legal obligations. It largely repeats what is already in binding air safety instruments and saying 'the same thing in a different way can actually weaken rather than strengthen the underlying norm because it adds additional grist to the interpretative mill'.[17]

The now widely accepted CUES is the only multilateral INCSEA type agreement agreed so far in the region. It is applicable to warships and

Building understandings and confidence 81

aircraft of WPNS navies. While there have been calls for the expansion of CUES to coast guards, regional coast guards have generally not supported this move. They point out that they have functions and responsibilities distinct from those of navies. They might use force as part of their day-to-day enforcement duties, but some of their tactics are listed as ones to be avoided under CUES, such as the simulation of attacks and the discharge of weapons. While most of the safety procedures set out in CUES are relevant to coast guards, they are less comfortable with the detailed communications procedures and manoeuvring instructions in the annexes to CUES. These are very 'naval' and arguably not relevant to coast guards. This discussion does not mean that coast guards don't need an appropriate document to prevent and manage the risks of incidents involving civil law enforcement vessels – given that many incidents in the region involve these vessels.

With submarines, the Singapore Navy has established a Safety Information Portal and is pushing for the adoption of an underwater CUES. These initiatives are aimed at improving confidence building to reduce the risks associated with accidents or incidents involving submarines.

The fundamental differences in the region regarding the EEZ has been an issue when dealing with the geographical area of application of MCBMs relating to the prevention and management of maritime incidents. For example, the US–China MOU-Rules notes that 'This memorandum is made without prejudice to either Side's policy perspective on military activities in the Exclusive Economic Zone'.[18] CUES attempted to avoid the issue but could not do so entirely.[19] CUES is a non-legally binding document.[20] It has unclear geographical application. While the earlier 2003 version of CUES applied to the high seas, territorial waters, contiguous zones, exclusive economic zones, and in archipelagic waters, CUES 2014 does not specify the maritime zones in which it operates.[21] However, it uses the definitions found in COLREGs, including the term 'at sea', which as used in COLREGs, indicates the high seas and 'all waters connected therewith navigable by seagoing vessels'.[22] Even though COLREGs entered into force before UNCLOS, it is clear that all navigable waters connected to the high seas, as expressed in COLREGs, would include territorial seas and the EEZ. It follows from this discussion that the geographical area of application of CUES is not entirely clear.

Ambiguities and uncertainties

Clarifying 'grey areas' in UNCLOS is a matter primarily of technical legal analysis and treaty interpretation but the process must also take account of the political and strategic reality of a situation. It is unlikely for example in current strategic circumstances that China will move from its current policy of requiring prior notification of the innocent passage of warships through its territorial sea. The geographical realities are, however, that there are few parts of the territorial sea of China through which a foreign warship might want to pass unless it was deviating from its normal route. A deviation by a foreign warship from its normal shipping route could well be seen as provocative, possibly suggesting 'non-innocent' passage. Furthermore, the collection of electronic intelligence could be 'an act aimed at collecting information to the prejudice of the defence or security of the coastal State' and therefore contrary to the right of innocent passage.[23]

The existing international legal framework is ill-equipped to support successful resolution of the regional disputes over freedoms of navigation. Root causes of problems with the law of the sea lie in basic conflicts of interest between regional counties, the 'built in' ambiguity of UNCLOS in several of its key regimes, the fact that the US is not a party to the convention, and the geographical complexity of the region that makes agreement of maritime boundaries very difficult.[24] As earlier chapters have discussed, there are many examples in the region of claims to maritime jurisdiction that appear inconsistent with the provisions of UNCLOS.

It has been claimed that 'UNCLOS lacks sensitivity towards the region's historical inter-sovereign and tributary relations, and ignores the traumatic colonial experiences of most Asian powers'.[25] It was unfortunate therefore that the members of the arbitral tribunal dealing with the case put by the Philippines to the special tribunal dealing with its case against China in the South China Sea were all Europeans with the sole exception of the president.[26] This adds to the risk that the findings of the tribunal may have reinforced views in the region about cultural bias in UNCLOS and international law more generally.

Another factor leading to growing distrust in the region over the last decade or so has been the 'damaging discourse of competing historical and legal claims over maritime territory'.[27] The Philippines and Vietnam have been particularly active in this 'war of words' with a fusillade of commentaries, reports and historical analyses aimed at discrediting China's claims in the South China Sea – even trying to change the name of the sea – to the East Sea in the case of Vietnam and the West Philippine Sea for the Philippines.[28] China has been losing this war, but in the long run, this does not matter as the relative merits of the separate claims to sovereignty will only be settled by negotiation, or when the results of extensive historical research are put before an independent arbitral tribunal set up to address the claims directly. Any of this is unlikely in the foreseeable future. In the meantime, the 'war of words' only adds to distrust, fuels nationalism and hinders cooperation.

Language issues

The language of the law of the sea is important in Southeast Asia. The S. Rajaratnam School of International Studies conducted a workshop in Singapore in March 2017 on ASEAN perspectives of the freedoms of navigation.[29] This noted how the phrase 'freedom of navigation' is a sensitive topic for some ASEAN states because they perceive the United States and others are using the phrase to push for extensive navigational freedoms contrary to their own sovereignty and jurisdiction. While they accept that 'freedoms of navigation' are inherently good and worthy, the archipelagic countries, in particular Indonesia and the Philippines, do not like the phrase because it implies a threat to the integrity of their national waters. They think of a 'right' of navigation rather than a 'freedom'. A 'right' has a more restrictive meaning than a 'freedom' – it is a qualified freedom. The difference may not be great in English, but it's more significant in Bahasa, where a 'freedom' is a *kebebasan* and a 'right' is a *hak*. A *kebebasan* is absolutely free, but a *hak* is a favour with the granter of the favour retaining the right to set conditions on it.

UNCLOS reflects this subtle distinction. It defines navigation in straits used for international navigation and the high seas as freedoms, whereas innocent passage in territorial seas and archipelagic waters, and transit along archipelagic sea lanes (ASLs) are 'rights'. Innocent passage is a 'right of navigation' rather than a 'freedom of navigation' because it has limitations and a coastal state can suspend the right in certain circumstances.

US Freedom of Navigation Program

UNCLOS was designed in part to halt the creeping jurisdiction of coastal states with some claiming a territorial sea beyond 12 nautical miles, emerging as the international norm prior to UNCLOS, and no agreement on the nature of the resources zone beyond the territorial sea. While that effort appears to have met with some success, many states are still purporting to extend their jurisdiction over their adjacent waters or to restrict navigational freedoms by a variety of means that seem neither consistent with UNCLOS nor with customary international law. The United States demonstrates its resistance to what it regards as excessive maritime claims through its Freedom of Navigation (FON) Program formally established in 1979. The program comprises a three-part complementary strategy to demonstrate its opposition to these excessive claims and to ensure that they do not become accepted as customary law with the passage of time. This strategy supports the global mobility of American forces and the unimpeded traffic of lawful commerce. It is the practical implementation of the American manifesto that 'the United States will fly, sail and operate wherever international law allows'.[30]

The Department of State leads the first part of the FON Program by diplomatically protesting an excessive maritime claim after it has been made by a coastal state. The Department of Defense provides the second part of the program by conducting operational challenges against excessive maritime claims. These operational challenges are usually referred to as Freedom of Navigation Operations (FONOPs). Not all claims judged by the United States to be excessive are followed by FONOPs – only those that are assessed as having a serious impact on freedoms of navigation. Bilateral and multilateral consultations are the third part of the program to promote adherence to UNCLOS and customary international law. These might occur, for example, to dissuade a country from introducing regulations or making a claim to jurisdiction that the United States regards as excessive.

The Department of Defense website on the FON program shows that the United States conducted FONOPs against 26 countries in 2018, of which about half were in the Asia-Pacific region, including China, Indonesia, Japan, the Philippines and Vietnam.[31] The excessive claims by China that were the target of a FONOP were: excessive straight baselines; jurisdiction over airspace above the EEZ; restriction on foreign aircraft flying through an Air Defence Identification Zone (ADIZ) without the intent to enter national airspace; domestic law criminalising survey activity by foreign entities in the EEZ, claiming security jurisdiction in the contiguous zone, and actions and statements that indicate a claim to a territorial sea around features not so entitled (i.e. low-tide elevations). This was a very lengthy list of claims much longer than that for any other country targeted by the FON program. Similar FONOPs aimed at claims by China have been made every year since 2009.

While the American FONOPs in the Asia-Pacific region in 2018 were mostly aimed against China's claims, the United States in publicising these operations, usually makes the point that China is not the only target of these operations. For example, after the USS *Curtis Wilbur* sailed near Triton Island in the Paracel group in 2016 challenging two claims by China in this group – the straight baselines claimed around these islands, and China's requirement for prior notification of a warship transiting its territorial sea, the US Department of Defense made an official statement claiming that the operation challenged attempts by all three claimants to these islands, China, Taiwan and Vietnam, to restrict navigational rights and freedoms.[32] However, despite the reference to Taiwan and Vietnam, the operation was clearly aimed at China, the current occupier of Triton Island, and the major target of American FONOPs in the South China Sea.

It is also only China that usually responds robustly to these operations often sending a warship to shadow the American vessel and invariably lodging a diplomatic protest.

FONOPs in the South China Sea

Over recent years, the United States has been conducting an escalating programme of FONOPs in the South China Sea after the Obama administration had put a stop to them from 2012 to 2015, with only a few in late 2015 and 2016, out of concern for upsetting China.[33] These operations can be categorised according to the type of claim being protested, and whether they are 'soft' or hard'. A 'hard' operation means one that is clearly aimed against China, particularly in the Spratly Islands or around Scarborough Shoal in the South China Sea, while 'soft' means a relatively less provocative routine navigational event, such as most FONOPs regularly carried out by the US Navy elsewhere in the world away from the South China Sea.

Initially the purpose of the American FONOPs in the South China Sea was unclear. This view was taken by several commentaries pointing out that confusion surrounded just what the United States was trying to achieve with its FONOPs.[34] Commentators pointed out that when the USS *Lassen* conducted a FONOP in late 2015 inside 12 nautical miles of Subi Reef and official reports referred to it as 'innocent passage', this was de facto recognition of China's claim to a territory that as a man-made structure on a low tide elevation was only entitled to a 500 metre zone.[35] This was not the message that Washington wanted to send with this operation. The implication was that it may have been better to go the full distance and go right in, conduct weapon practices, operate helicopters and so on, simply to demonstrate that it was not innocent passage through a territorial sea. But of course, the United States was unlikely to do that.

Judgments by the arbitral tribunal in the case between the Philippines and China in the South China Sea have helped to clarify just what the United States is trying to achieve with FONOPs in the area. The tribunal determined that they are no true 'islands' in the Spratlys entitled to a full suite of maritime zones – only 'rocks' entitled only to a territorial sea and contiguous zone, and 'low tide elevations' that are submerged at high tide and, even if they have been built up as artificial islands, they are entitled at most to a 500 metre safety zone in accordance with UNCLOS Article 60.

The FONOPs now being conducted by the United States in the South China Sea fall into the following broad categories of challenges:

- Against the requirement for prior notification or authorisation of the transit of foreign warships through the territorial sea. Several countries

86 *Building understandings and confidence*

bordering the South China Sea have this requirement. The FONOP is conducted by sailing without notice through the territorial sea. However, it should be noted that no country claiming sovereignty over features in the Spratlys has actually claimed a territorial sea around the features it claims. Thus the United States when conducting such a FONOP is omitting the first part of the FON Program, because there has been nothing formal to protest.

- Against presumed claims, notably by China, to a 12-nautical mile territorial sea around a low-tide elevation even though it may have been built up as an artificial island. The FONOP is conducted by sailing within the 12-mile limit and exercising or operating helicopters contrary to the right of innocent passage. It is aimed at showing that the feature as a low tide elevation is not entitled to a territorial sea.
- Against excessive territorial sea straight baselines, notably those by China around the Paracel islands. The FONOP is conducted by warships sailing through the group without prior notification and when outside the 12-nautical mile limit around the larger islands in the group, which are likely to be full 'islands', conducting operations contrary to the right of innocent passage. For example, Figure 4.1 shows a possible FONOP through the Paracels.[36] This figure shows the territorial sea straight baselines claimed by China around the Paracels, a typical route through the Paracels used by merchant ships transiting between Hong Kong/southern China and the Singapore Strait, and the possible route by an American warship conducting a FONOP.

FONOPs in or around the Paracels tend to be 'soft' operations because they can involve a ship transiting along a well-used shipping lane past a naturally formed feature. China only challenges the right of foreign warships to pass through the group. Commercial vessels transiting through the Paracels pass well within 12 nautical miles of various features in the group. I did so myself several years ago when travelling in a large container ship from Hong Kong to Port Klang in Malaysia. There were other merchant ships at the time doing likewise. Over the years, warships of various countries, including the United States, have probably also done so without being challenged by China. It is an established shipping route between Guangzhou and Hong Kong in the north and Singapore Straits in the south, and China has made no attempt to exercise control over foreign merchant ships using the route. Presumably because of these considerations, China's response to FONOPs in the Paracels can be more muted than its responses in the Spratlys.

In comparison, FONOPs in the Spratlys might be seen as 'hard' (i.e. relatively more provocative and contentious) because the ships involved

Building understandings and confidence 87

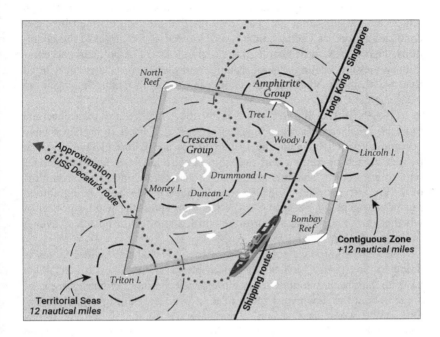

Figure 4.1 FONOPs in the Paracel Islands.

deliberately leave any established shipping route to demonstrate a right of innocent passage in these hotly disputed waters. As such, it is open to question whether they are in fact exercising a right of innocent passage because in contravention of UNCLOS Article 18(2) their passage is not 'continuous and expeditious', as well as arguably 'prejudicial to the peace, good order or security of the coastal State' in contravention of UNCLOS Article 19(2). Except in the South China Sea, American FONOPS are usually given little publicity. The publicity now being given by Washington to these events in the South China looks like an intentional effort to demonstrate that the United States is pushing back against China in the region.

American FONOPs in the South China Sea have led to a security dilemma between the United States and China. This is characterised by strategic distrust and an apparent action–reaction dynamic in which initiatives on one side are being driven by the actions of the other. The FONOPs have only fuelled this security dilemma and added to the militarisation of the South China Sea. While the United States claims to be not taking sides in the sovereignty claims, its FONOPs in the South China Sea send a political message that can easily be misconstrued. Even though American warships may sail past features that are also claimed by other countries as well as China, China is still viewed as the target of the operations. That is how most people in the region see it. The political and community view in Beijing, Hanoi, Manila and elsewhere is that the United States with its FONOPs against claims in the South China Sea is taking sides against China.

FONOPs in the South China Sea by the United States have become more political actions rather than assertions of a legal right. They have become a 'game' between the United States and China. The Americans publicise each operation, and the Chinese respond in a familiar manner with foreign policy statements and occasional shadowing and warning off of the American vessel. FONOPS are all about the US Navy being able to sail its warships wherever it likes rather than about the legal question of whether or not particular features are entitled to a territorial sea or even a full suite of maritime zones.

There are significant political downsides to what the United States is doing in the South China Sea. Misperceptions about American FONOPs have already been mentioned, but more generally, other countries are concerned about the downward spiral of trust between Beijing and Washington. In the worst case scenario, they are fearful that if current trends continue they will be forced to take sides with either China or the United States. Also, Indonesia has strongly criticised the FONOPs,[37] while Malaysian Prime Minister Mahathir Mohamad has lamented the increased naval activity in the South China Sea saying 'I think there should not be too many warships. Warships create tension'.[38] Japan has declined to participate in formal FONOPs, and even Australia, as Washington's loyalist supporter in the region, has backed off from joining the FONOPs.

The United Kingdom has undertaken one formal FONOP in the South China Sea. In August 2018, the amphibious ship HMS *Albion* passed through or near the Paracel islands. The ship may not have passed within 12 nautical miles of any feature and the operation was more a demonstration against China's enclosure of this group with territorial sea straight baselines.[39] Australia, France, India and Japan have all had warships operating in the South China Sea demonstrating a general freedom to operate in the sea but have not undertaken formal FONOPS. Even so, their movements are frequently shadowed by Chinese naval units.[40]

Despite the rhetoric about preserving general freedoms of navigation in the South China Sea and the importance of seaborne trade across this sea, the American FONOPs in the area are all about preserving the rights of warships to pass through a claimed territorial sea without prior notification or authorisation. To a lesser extent, they are about protesting China's

Building understandings and confidence 89

excessive claims to a territorial sea around the various features it occupies in the sea. They are not achieving anything in terms of preserving the freedoms of navigation by commercial vessels in the South China Sea. These are not disputed or threatened by China.

Taiwan Strait

As relations between China and the United States deteriorated during the early months of 2019 and their trade war escalated, the Taiwan Strait between Taiwan and the mainland of China became the location of a fresh round of their differences over freedoms of navigation. In the first five months of 2019 alone, American warships transited the Taiwan Strait on five occasions provoking strong responses from China on each occasion.[41] In a separate incident in April 2019, China withdrew its invitation for a French warship to attend its fleet review in Qingdao after the vessel had made a publicised transit of the Taiwan Strait.[42] These incidents look like providing another example of how higher level political and strategic tensions can impact on freedoms of navigation.

The Taiwan Strait connects the South China Sea with the East China Sea and has an average width of about 180 km or about 100 nautical miles. It is an important route for commercial shipping, mainly for coastal Chinese shipping, ships travelling between Hong Kong and Northeast Asia, and between Southeast Asia and northern China and Japan.[43] Much more shipping uses the Luzon Strait between Taiwan and the Philippines.

The regime of transit passage through straits used for international navigation in UNCLOS Part III does not apply to the Taiwan Strait in view of its width. As discussed in Chapter 2, this regime was introduced as a consequence of increasing the width of the territorial sea to 12 nautical miles and enclosing more international straits as the territorial sea of the littoral state(s). To argue that the transit passage regime applies to the Taiwan Strait, and other international straits not fully enclosed as territorial sea, would set up anomalies between UNCLOS Part III and the EEZ regime, notably by having the transit passage rules such as those regarding the duties of ships and aircraft during transit passage in UNCLOS Article 39 apply to the EEZ more generally. There is an EEZ corridor running through the Taiwan Strait to which high seas freedoms, subject to the limitations noted in Chapter 3, apply rather than the more limited nature of the transit passage regime.[44]

China is clearly very sensitive about activities in the Taiwan Strait. Under the 'one state' regime, it regards the entire Taiwan Strait as its own EEZ and subject to its claimed restrictions over military activities within those waters. It is also relevant that China declared straight territorial baselines along its mainland coast in 1996 which the United States regards as excessive. These have the impact of pushing China's territorial sea further out into the strait than is legally justifiable. China would also like foreign warships to use the Luzon Strait perhaps by using the alternative strait argument in UNCLOS Article 36 that excludes straits from the transit passage regime if a route exists through the high seas or through an EEZ of similar convenience with respect to navigational and hydrographical characteristics. But as has been noted, the transit passage regime does not apply to the Taiwan Strait.

In the past foreign warships have transited the strait without complaint from China provided they did not enter China's territorial sea. However, in an incident reported in the Australian media in April 2001, Australian warships were challenged by a Chinese warship during a passage through the Taiwan Strait but their right to do so was defended by the Australian Prime Minister on the grounds that 'the Australian warships were engaged in what was called "innocent passage" through the territorial waters of another country'.[45] If the Australian vessels did in fact pass through the Chinese territorial sea, when navigationally it was not necessary for them to do so, and they were engaged in intelligence collection activities, then it was not innocent passage.

The confrontations in the Taiwan Strait in 2019 may be another manifestation of the growing strategic tensions between China and the United States. Washington publicises these transits with the implication that they are somehow contrary to China's regulations and China responds in a predictable manner. China's claimed justification for objecting to the transits is not entirely clear but could be because the ships pass through China's EEZ and China suspects that they are conducting intelligence collection or carrying out 'military surveys', which of course they could be.

Conclusions

This book has reviewed strategic, political and legal issues with freedoms of navigation in the Asia-Pacific region. It has highlighted problems with interpreting the general law of the sea as set out in UNCLOS and with the effectiveness of this Convention as the foundation for a regional maritime security regime with established principles for the freedoms of navigation in the region. There are problems in dealing with matters that UNCLOS is silent upon, such as the prior notification of warship transit in the territorial sea and military activities in the EEZ; and in implementing the general international rules embodied in UNCLOS both at a regional level and in a meaningful operational manner. Problems of implementation arise, for example, with identifying and delineating ASLs, and with applying the 'burden sharing' principles for transit passage as set out in UNCLOS Article 43. While states will generally argue that their position is consistent with UNCLOS and customary law, divergent positions clearly do exist and while this is the case, there is potential for tension and even conflict.

There has been much talk in recent years of the importance of maintaining the global rules-based order as though there is a single and universally agreed system.[46] Since the end of World War Two, this global system has been important in maintaining relations between states and reducing tensions. The international rules-based order of the seas is an important element of this system, but like the main over-arching order, it is seen as under threat. This threat is perceived as coming primarily from China with its assertive behaviour in the South China Sea and elsewhere, as well as its failure to accept the judgments of the arbitral tribunal dealing with the case brought against it by the Philippines on South China Sea issues. However, lesser powers in the Asia-Pacific region, such as Indonesia, Malaysia and the Philippines, are also taking actions and expressing views that throw doubt on whether there are still universally agreed freedoms of navigation.

None of this is to suggest a need to amend UNCLOS, and, in any case, it would be difficult to obtain the necessary consensus in the contemporary world. Changes to the law of the sea occur through new international instruments,[47] and evolving customary law rather than through amendments to UNCLOS. Amendment of UNCLOS is possible under UNCLOS Article 312 whereby a State Party may request the convening of a conference to consider proposed amendments, and provided not less than one half of the States Parties reply favourably to the request, the UN Secretary-General can convene the conference. However, getting such agreement from over half of the State Parties would be difficult in the contemporary world.

New law of the sea is being talked about, for example, to respond to scientific discoveries such as with the need for a management regime for the living resources of the deep sea bed ('archaea'), or to deal with emerging environmental concerns such as the conservation and sustainable use of marine biological diversity of areas beyond national jurisdiction. In the context of freedoms of navigation, changes might be required in response to technological developments. With advances in surveillance and detection systems, the oceans and seas of the world are becoming transparent. The movements of surface warships can no longer be kept secret and from a navigational safety point of view, it is often no longer appropriate that they should try to hide their identity. After several serious accidents caused partly by warships not showing their automatic identification system (AIS) details, the US Navy and other navies are now requiring their ships to show AIS data in busy shipping lanes.[48]

The growing use of unmanned or autonomous vehicles at sea is another development that may impact on freedoms of navigation. Conventional legal wisdom suggests that autonomous ships and unmanned surface vehicles (USVs) should be regarded as 'ships' and unmanned underwater vehicles (UUVs) as 'submarines'.[49] However, operationally it may not be that easy. UUVs, in particular, will be attractive vehicles for covert surveillance and intelligence collection and may be used for that purpose in foreign EEZs and territorial seas without necessarily conforming to the accepted freedoms of navigation associated with submarines. For example, it will be difficult for a UUV operating in another country's territorial sea to travel on the surface and show its flag as required by UNCLOS Article 20 despite this article already referring to 'other underwater vehicles'.

A key area of possible further research is the analysis of state practice with the law of the sea in East Asian seas. There are many examples of where state practice in the region appears to be diverging from the conventional and traditional law of the sea. Examples include the use of territorial sea straight baselines and claims to deny rights of navigation and overflight beyond the limits of the territorial sea. We are yet to see whether this state practice will subsequently gain legitimacy and acceptance as customary law. Suffice to note, however, that we are dealing with issues where the United States, as the principal guardian of the traditional law of the sea through its publication of excessive claims and the FON program, may already be falling behind what is emerging state practice. And as was noted in Chapter 3, it would seem that the United States does not accept some parts of the EEZ regime as customary international law.

Several specific conclusions stand out from the discussion in this book. First, at the heart of the disputes over freedoms of navigation in the region are the escalating tensions between China and the United States. The military establishments of both countries appear to be preparing for war with each other. While some MCBMs are in place to mitigate the risks of incidents between their maritime forces, the risks will not be fully reduced until their bilateral relationship is improved. Any common ground between them on freedoms of navigation is unlikely while the United States remains steadfast in its liberal interpretations of the freedoms of navigation and China seeks maximum control over its adjacent waters. Both will have to compromise to some extent. It has sometimes been suggested that as China becomes a global maritime power, it may liberalise its position on key freedoms of navigation by for example, dropping its claimed restrictions on foreign military activities in its EEZ, but that is unlikely given China's history of foreign domination and fear of foreign encirclement. As Henry Kissinger has pointed out, the game of *wei qi* (or 'Go') and the fear of strategic encirclement play a key role in Chinese strategic thinking.[50]

The second broad conclusion is that many disputes over freedoms of navigation in the region are associated with the EEZ regime, particularly with regard to what military activities are acceptable in another country's EEZ. This is one area where practical MCBMs should be possible, but while, as discussed in Chapter 3, the OPRF in Japan has done a lot of work in developing prospective common understandings, its recommendations have not been considered by any Track One forum. Over the years CSCAP has also done much work aimed at seeking common understandings of law of the sea issues,[51] but again this work has not received any serious consideration in Track One forums. Deeply held political positions and strategic perspectives of key regional stakeholders are barriers to such consideration. Real progress with resolving the different perspectives of key freedom of navigation issues will only be achieved when some major Track One regional forum is prepared to address them. Unfortunately in current strategic circumstances, the main protagonists, China and the United States, are likely to continue blocking such consideration. This has certainly been my personal experience.

Third, despite all the generalised rhetoric about the importance of freedoms of navigation in the region, it is clear that the only freedoms that are under threat are those applicable to naval vessels. Many regional countries are sensitive to the activities of foreign warships in their adjacent waters. The freedoms of navigation of commercial vessels are not under threat, except in the limited circumstances of coastal states seeking additional controls over shipping in their adjacent waters on environmental grounds. Seaborne trade is hugely significant in the Asia-Pacific region and China is a major stakeholder in that trade. It is unreasonable to think that it would place restrictions on the freedoms of navigation of commercial vessels.

A fourth conclusion relates to the navigational regimes in UNCLOS. As shipping traffic increases in key international straits and through archipelagos in the region, the littoral states concerned are likely to seek more controls over transiting shipping mainly on environmental grounds. As was the case when Australia introduced compulsory pilotage in the Torres Strait, these new controls will draw objections from major powers, and if costs are involved, from ship-owning associations. The littoral states, particularly the archipelagic states and those adjacent to straits used for international navigation, may also seek ways and means of recovering the costs of providing services to transiting ships, such as hydrographic services and navigational aids, as well as the costs of protection against marine pollution. Again these measures will likely draw opposition from commercial interests, as well as from some major powers on the strategic grounds that they hamper or impair the right of transit passage in contravention of UNCLOS Article 42(2) that applies also to ASL passage through Article 54.

Fifth, some of the disputes over freedoms of navigation in the region arise or are aggravated because some key concepts get 'lost in translation'. Indonesia and the Philippines, in particular, are sensitive to other countries talking about 'freedoms of navigation' in their waters. They see this as an affront to their sovereignty and sovereign rights. Also, in the context of the EEZ regime, 'sovereignty' and 'sovereign rights' can be confusing concepts, particularly when, as noted in Chapter 3, they translate as the same thing in some regional languages. When China, for example, is alleged to claim 'indisputable sovereignty' over parts of the South China Sea, it may, in fact, just be claiming 'indisputable sovereign rights', which is much less objectionable. In my experience with CSCAP and other regional forums, these language issues occur frequently when drafting meeting statements or agreements. They are potentially an area for further research. Clearer agreed understandings of key concepts with freedoms of navigation could be an important MCBM.

Lastly, the time has probably come when the major maritime powers should rethink their opposition to the requirement of some regional countries for prior notification of the transit of foreign warships through their territorial sea. This would constitute a significant MCBM. Arguably not giving prior notification is no longer necessary to protect the security of warship movements since these movements may already be known by other means, such as by effective coastal surveillance systems or if the warships are showing AIS. The benefits of this move as an MCBM may outweigh any costs as a result of the secrecy of naval movements being lost. It would also assure a coastal state that the intentions of a foreign warship heading towards its territorial sea were peaceful. This conclusion applies only to the requirement for prior notification and not to the requirement for prior authorisation which is much more objectionable.

Final thoughts

There is a close intersection between international law and politics. At the end of the day, it is politics not the law that will resolve many disputes we see at present with the law of the sea. It is also politics that condition the evolution of different perspectives of the law of the sea, including the freedoms of navigation. Just over 30 years ago, Australia, the United States and others were still regarding the Java Sea as 'high seas' with absolute freedoms of navigation and overflight. But now they are under the full sovereignty of Indonesia as archipelagic waters subject to the regimes of ASL and innocent passage. Indonesia robustly defends this sovereignty, even by declaring an ADIZ over parts of the Java Sea. All this just shows how the excessive claims of yesterday can become the customary law of today. But it is, of course, this advance of the law that the United States is seeking to oppose with its FON program.

All this 'lawfare' and 'war of words' over freedoms of navigation in the region is not helpful. It is leading nowhere other than down the path of increasing distrust, misunderstanding, and regional instability. Political suspicions are still rife in the Asia-Pacific region, in East Asia in particular, and the region lacks the strong political frameworks that could facilitate cooperative clearer understandings of freedoms of navigation in the region, as well as appropriate MCBMs.

Uncertainty in the law of sea may grow, and the United States, in particular, may find increasing difficulty in maintaining its strict interpretation of navigational regimes and coastal state jurisdiction. This uncertainty is most evident at a regional level in East Asia but has global implications. East Asia will be critical in shaping developments with the international law of the sea of the future. In doing so, state practice in this theatre, under the influence of nationalistic domestic politics and regional tensions, may well diverge from the orthodox, largely Western view of the customary law of the sea. The law of the sea has already had to change significantly in recent decades to meet the needs of new key stakeholder nations, especially those in East Asia, such as Indonesia and increasingly China, which have been active in defining the contemporary law of the sea.

UNCLOS was a magnificent achievement for the 1970s and 1980s and remains a careful balance of the rights and duties of the different categories of State. However, its limitations must also be appreciated, particularly with freedoms of navigation. A challenge in building security and stability in the Asia-Pacific region, where maritime issues are so important, is to recognise the limitations of UNCLOS and to negotiate a regional consensus on aspects of the Convention that are less than clear or where differences of view exist. Strategic and political issues drive these different views and it is these factors that in turn will influence the future law of the sea. As Ken Booth observed in his seminal work *Law, Force and Diplomacy at Sea*, 'the changing law of the sea is too serious to be left to international lawyers'.[52]

Notes

1 Sam Bateman, 'The Compulsory Pilotage Regime in the Torres Strait – A "Melting Pot" of Operational, Legal, and Political Considerations' in Aldo Chircop, Ted L. McDorman and Susan J. Rolston (eds), *The Future of Ocean Regime-Building – Essays in Tribute to Douglas M. Johnston*, Leiden: Martinus Nijhoff Publishers, 2009, pp. 261–286.

2 Robin R. Churchill, 'Levels of Implementation of the Law of the Sea Convention: An Overview' in Davor Vidas and Willy Ostreng (eds), *Order for the Oceans at the Turn of the Century*, Dordrecht: The Fridtjof Nansen Institute, 1999, p. 323.
3 Commonwealth of Australia, *Australian Maritime Doctrine – RAN Doctrine 1*, Canberra: Sea Power Centre Australia, 2010, pp. 72–73.
4 Harry J. Kazianis, 'Air-Sea Battle's Next Step: JAM-GC on Deck', *The National Interest*, 25 November 2015, https://nationalinterest.org/feature/air-sea-battles-next-step-jam-gc-deck-14440.
5 Marcus Warren, 'Japan sinks "North Korea spying ship"', *Telegraph*, 24 December 2001, www.telegraph.co.uk/news/worldnews/asia/northkorea/1366227/Japan-sinks-North-Korea-spying-ship.html.
6 Jon M. Van Dyke, 'Transit Passage through International Straits' in Chircop et al., *The Future of Ocean Regime-Building*, p. 196.
7 Sam Bateman, 'The Compulsory Pilotage Regime in the Torres Strait'.
8 James Kraska, 'Confidence Building Measures to Facilitate Navigation in the South China Sea', *The International Journal of Marine and Coastal Law*, Vol. 32, 2017, p. 294.
9 Department of Political and Security Council Affairs, United Nations Centre for Disarmament, Report of the Secretary-General, *Comprehensive Study on Confidence-building Measures*, New York: United Nations, 1982.
10 Sam Bateman, 'Background Paper: Maritime Confidence building measures – an overview' in 'Maritime Confidence Building Measures in the South China Sea Conference', *Special Report*, No. 55, Canberra: Australian Strategic Policy Institute, September 2013, pp. 7–12.
11 Sam Bateman, 'Maritime Confidence and Security Building Measures in the Asian Pacific Region and the Law of the Sea' in James Crawford and Donald R. Rothwell (eds), *The Law of the Sea in the Asian Pacific Region*, Dordrecht: Martinus Nijhof, 1995, pp. 223–236.
12 Nien-Tsu Alfred Hu and James K. Oliver, 'A Framework for Small Navy Theory: The 1982 UN Law of the Sea Convention', *Naval War College Review*, Vol. 41, Spring 1988, p. 44.
13 Mark J. Valencia, 'Law of the Sea in Transition: Navigational Nightmare for the Maritime Powers?' *Journal of Maritime Law and Commerce*, Vol. 18, No. 4, 1987, p. 542.
14 Jin-Hyun Paik, 'Enhancing Maritime Security in Asia' in Dalchoong Kim and Jing-Hoon Lee (eds), *Comprehensive Security – Conceptions and Realities in Asia*, Seoul: Yonsei University Press, 2000, p. 101.
15 The ARF Concept Paper on preventive diplomacy and confidence-building is available on the ARF website at: http://aseanregionalforum.asean.org/files/library/Terms%20of%20References%20and%20Concept%20Papers/Concept%20Paper%20of%20ARF.pdf.
16 Shannon Tiezzi, 'No More Dangerous Intercepts for US, China Military Aircraft?', *The Diplomat*, 25 September 2015, https://thediplomat.com/2015/09/no-more-dangerous-intercepts-for-us-china-miltary-aircraft/.
17 James Kraska and Raul 'Pete' Pedrozo, 'The US–China Arrangement for Air-to-Air Encounters Weakens International Law', *Lawfare*, 9 March 2016, www.lawfareblog.com/us-china-arrangement-air-air-encounters-weakens-international-law.
18 US–China Memorandum of Understanding on the Rules of Behavior for the Safety of Air and Maritime Encounters (MOU-Rules), signed 9–10 November

2014, Section V, http://archive.defense.gov/pubs/141112_MemorandumOf UnderstandingRegardingRules.pdf.
19 Anh Duc Ton, 'Code for Unplanned Encounters at Sea and its Practical Limitations in the East and South China Seas', *Australian Journal of Maritime and Ocean Affairs*, Vol. 9, No. 4, 2017, pp. 227–239.
20 *Code for Unplanned Encounters at Sea*, www.jag.navy.mil/distrib/instructions/ CUES_2014.pdf.
21 Ton, 'Code for Unplanned Encounters at Sea', pp. 230–231.
22 *Convention on the International Regulations for Preventing Collisions at Sea* 1972 (COLREGS), www.jag.navy.mil/distrib/instructions/COLREG-1972.pdf. Rule 1(a) of COLREGS states that 'These Rules shall apply to all vessels upon the high seas and in all waters connected therewith navigable by seagoing vessels'.
23 UNCLOS Article 19(2)(c).
24 Sam Bateman, 'Maritime Boundary Delimitation, Excessive Claims and Effective Regime Building in the South China Sea', in Yann-huei Song and Keyuan Zou (eds), *Major Law and Policy Issues in the South China Sea – European and American Perspectives*, Farnham: Ashgate, 2013, pp. 119–136.
25 Kun-Chin Lin and Andres Villar Gertner, 'Maritime Security in the Asia-Pacific – China and the Emerging Order in the East and South China Seas', Research Paper, London: Chatham House – the Royal Institute of International Affairs, July 2015, p. 22.
26 The five-member Arbitral Tribunal was chaired by Judge Thomas A. Mensah of Ghana. The other Members were Judge Jean-Pierre Cot of France, Judge Stanislaw Pawlak of Poland, Professor Alfred Soons of the Netherlands, and Judge Rüdiger Wolfrum of Germany. Permanent Court of Arbitration (PCA), Arbitration between the Republic of the Philippines and the People's Republic of China: 'Arbitral Tribunal Establishes Rules of Procedure and Initial Timetable', *PCA Press Release*, 27 August 2013, www.pca-cpa.org/PH-CN%20 -%20Press%20Release%20(ENG)%2020130827e141.pdf?fil_id=2311.
27 Lin and Gertner, 'Maritime Security in the Asia-Pacific, p. 9.
28 For example, Justice Antonio T. Carpio, 'The Rule of Law in the West Philippine Sea Dispute', *Manila Bulletin*, 6 September 2013, www.mb.com.ph/the-rule-of-law-in-the-west-philippine-sea-dispute/ (accessed 11 September 2013); and Carl Thayer, 'Lawfare or Warfare?: History, International Law and Geo-Strategy', *The Diplomat*, 4 July 2014, http://thediplomat.com/2014/07/lawfare-or-warfare-history-international-law-and-geo-strategy/.
29 Philipp Martin Dingeldey, rapporteur, 'Understanding Freedoms of Navigation – ASEAN Perspectives', *Event Report*, 7 March 2017, www.rsis.edu.sg/rsis-publication/idss/understanding-freedoms-of-navigation-asean-perspectives/#. WpN5S-RG34s.
30 Don Emmerson, 'Matching Power with Purpose in the South China Sea: A Proposal', *AMTI Update*, 28 November 2017, https://amti.csis.org/matching-power-purpose-south-china-sea.
31 US Department of Defense, *Annual Freedom of Navigation Report Fiscal Year 2018*, https://policy.defense.gov/Portals/11/Documents/FY18%20DoD%20 Annual%20FON%20Report%20(final).pdf?ver=2019-03-19-103517-010.
32 Sam LaGrone, 'U.S. Destroyer Challenges More Chinese South China Sea Claims in New Freedom of Navigation Operation', *USNI News*, 30 January 2016, http://news.usni.org/2016/01/30/u-s-destroyer-challenges-more-chinese-south-china-sea-claims-in-new-freedom-of-navigation-operation.

98 *Building understandings and confidence*

33 Kristina Wong, 'EXCLUSIVE: Trump's Pentagon Plans to Challenge Chinese Claims in South China Sea', *Breitbart News*, 20 July 2017, www.breitbart.com/national-security/2017/07/20/trump-pentagon-south-china-sea-plan/.
34 Sam LaGrone, 'Confusion Continues to Surround U.S. South China Sea Freedom of Navigation Operation', *USNI News*, 5 November 2015, http://news.usni.org/2015/11/05/confusion-continues-to-surround-u-s-south-china-sea-freedom-of-navigation-operation.
35 Captain Anthony Cowden USN, 'Opinion: USS Lassen's Transit of Subi Reef Was Not So "Innocent"', *USNI News*, 5 November 2015, http://news.usni.org/2015/11/04/opinion-uss-lassens-transit-of-subi-reef-was-not-so-innocent; and Adam Klein and Mira Rapp-Hooper, 'What Did the Navy Do in the South China Sea', *Lawfare*, 5 November 2015, www.lawfareblog.com/what-did-navy-do-south-china-sea.
36 This figure is based on US State Department, 'Straight Baselines Claim: China', *Limits in the Seas No. 117*, 9 July 1996. It includes an approximate route of a USN ship on a FONOP through the Paracels from Eleanor Freund, *Freedom of Navigation in the South China Sea: A Practical Guide*, Belfer Center for Science and International Affairs, Harvard Kennedy School, June 2017, p. 38.
37 Daniel Moss, 'Indonesia Calls for US–China to "Restrain Themselves", Lashes US "Power Projection" after Spratly Sail-by', *South China Morning Post*, 28 October 2015, www.scmp.com/news/china/diplomacy-defence/article/1873456/indonesia-calls-us-china-restrain-themselves-lashes-us?page=all.
38 Bhavan Jaipragas, 'Forget the Warships: Malaysian PM Mahathir's Peace Formula for South China Sea', *South China Morning Post*, 19 June 2018, www.scmp.com/week-asia/geopolitics/article/2151403/forget-warships-malaysian-pm-mahathirs-peace-formula-south.
39 Tim Kelly, 'Exclusive: British Navy Warship Sails near South China Sea Islands, Angering Beijing', *Reuters*, 6 September 2018, www.reuters.com/article/us-britain-china-southchinasea-exclusive/exclusive-british-navy-warship-sails-near-south-china-sea-islands-angering-beijing-idUSKCN1LM017.
40 Andrew Greene, 'Australian Ships Tailed by Chinese Military in South China Sea', *ABC News*, 27 May 2019, www.abc.net.au/news/2019-05-27/indo-pacific-endeavour-chinese-ships-exercise-sea/11153874.
41 Allen Cone, 'Two US Navy Ships Pass through Taiwan Strait as Tensions with China Rise', *UPI*, 24 May 2019, www.upi.com/Defense-News/2019/05/24/Two-US-Navy-ships-pass-through-Taiwan-Strait-as-tensions-with-China-rise/2011558706713/.
42 Ankit Panda, 'Making Sense of China's Reaction to the French Navy's Taiwan Strait Transit', *The Diplomat*, 27 April 2019, https://thediplomat.com/2019/04/making-sense-of-chinas-reaction-to-the-french-navys-taiwan-strait-transit/.
43 Joseph Morgan and Mark J. Valencia (eds), *Atlas for Marine Policy in East Asian Seas*, Berkeley: University of California Press, 1992, Map – Shipping and Specialised Maritime Regimes, p. 148.
44 James Kraska, *Maritime Power and the Law of the Sea*, New York: Oxford University Press, 2011, pp. 126–127.
45 Ian Henderson, 'Navy Row Threatens China Ties', *The Australian*, 30 April 2001, p. 1.
46 For example, the United Kingdom's 2018 National Security Capability Review makes 14 references to the 'international rules-based order', 'rules-based

Building understandings and confidence 99

system', 'rules-based international order', 'rules-based international system', 'international rules-based system' or 'multilateral rules-based system'. As quoted in Malcolm Chalmers, 'Which Rules? Why there is no Single 'Rules-Based International System"', *RUSI Occasional Paper*, London: Royal United Services Institute (RUSI), April 2019, note 2, p. 1.

47 The prime examples of new instruments are the two supplementary agreements agreed soon after UNCLOS was open for signature: the 1994 *Agreement relating to the implementation of Part XI of UNCLOS*, and the 1995 *Agreement for the Implementation of the Provisions of UNCLOS relating to the Conservation and Management of Straddling Fish Stocks and Highly Migratory Fish Stocks.*

48 Sam Bateman, 'US Naval Accidents Revisited', *The Interpreter*, 21 May 2018, www.lowyinstitute.org/the-interpreter/us-naval-accidents-revisited.

49 Kraska, *Maritime Power and the Law of the Sea*, pp. 282–283.

50 Henry Kissinger, *On China*, New York: Penguin Books, 2012, pp. 23–25.

51 For example, CSCAP Memorandum No. 6 – The Practice of the Law of the Sea in the Asia Pacific (December 2002), and CSCAP Memorandum No. 12 – Guidelines for Maritime Cooperation in Enclosed and Semi-Enclosed Seas and Similar Sea Areas of the Asia Pacific (July 2008). These memoranda are available on the CSCAP website at: www.cscap.org/.

52 Ken Booth, *Law, Force and Diplomacy at Sea*, London: Allen and Unwin, 1985, p. 5.

Index

ADIZ *see* Air Defence Identification Zone
Aids to Navigation Fund 36
Air Defence Identification Zone 84, 95
AIS *see* automatic identification system
ANCORS *see* Australian National Centre for Ocean Resources and Security
archipelagic sea lanes 14, 37–42, 45–7, 83; designation of 38, 41–2; passage 16, 37–9; regimes of 47, 94
ARF *see* ASEAN Regional Forum
ASEAN 18–19, 71, 79, 83; states 83; trade statistics 18
ASEAN Regional Forum 71, 79, 83
Asia-Pacific region 1–3, 19–20, 37, 46, 66, 69–70, 76–7, 79, 84, 90–1, 93, 95
'Asian Group' 15
ASLs *see* archipelagic sea lanes
Association of Southeast Asian Nations *see* ASEAN
Austin, Greg 19
Australia 10, 17–18, 29, 33, 35, 39, 41, 77–8, 88, 93–4; Defence White Paper 18–19; eastern 19; and the EEZ 66; exports 19; government of 17; and the "innocent passage" through the territorial waters of another country 90; introduces compulsory pilotage in the Torres Strait 76; northwest 10, 41; overseas trade 19; warships 90
Australian Defence White Paper 18–19
automatic identification system 91, 94

Bawean Island (north of Bali) 41

Beijing 12–13, 69, 88
Belfer Center 59
Belt and Road Initiative 12
Booth, Ken 58, 95
BRI *see* Belt and Road Initiative

Cambodia 4, 6, 26, 29
'Castaneda Compromise' 56
CBMs *see* confidence-building measures
Center for Strategic and International Studies 18
Cheju Island 32, 34
Cheju Strait 32, 34, 78
China 1–4, 6–7, 9–12, 15, 17–20, 26–7, 29, 32–4, 60–1, 66, 69, 77–8, 80, 82, 84–95; claims of sovereignty 12; criticised by the Arbitral Tribunal in The Hague 12; and the EEZ 66, 90; fighter aircraft 66; history of foreign domination and fear 92; maritime surveillance aircraft in the Yellow Sea 66; patrol vessels 66; position on military activities in an EEZ 61; protecting claims to a territorial sea around areas it occupies 88–9; requirement for prior notification of a warship transiting its territorial sea 26, 84; response to FONOPs in the Paracels 86; southern 19, 43; and the *USNS Impeccable* incident 66–7, 69
Churchill, R.R. 28, 34, 76
CLCS *see* Commission on the Limits of the Continental Shelf
Code for Unplanned Encounters between Ships 80–1

Index

COLREGs *see* International Regulations for Preventing Collisions at Sea
Commission on the Limits of the Continental Shelf 11
confidence-building measures 78–81, 92–5
confrontations in the Taiwan Strait (2019) 90
Congressional Research Service 59–60
Cooperative Mechanism for Safety of Navigation and Environment Protection in the Straits of Malacca and Singapore 36–7
Council for Security Cooperation in the Asia Pacific 10, 93, 94
CRS *see* Congressional Research Service
CSCAP *see* Council for Security Cooperation in the Asia Pacific
CSIS *see* Center for Strategic and International Studies
CUES *see* Code for Unplanned Encounters between Ships
customary law 35, 76, 83, 91–2, 95

Diaoyu islands 10
dispute resolution procedures 69, 91
distant water fishing nation 6
Dokdo islands 10
domestic politics 2, 95; *see also* politics
Dona Paz inter-island ferry disaster 43
due regard principle 57–9, 70
DWFN *see* distant water fishing nation

East Asia 2–9, 15–19, 25, 28–9, 34, 37, 46, 58, 67, 78–9, 95; archipelagic chain of 6–7; and 'creeping sovereignty' issues 14; and links to the Middle East and Europe by the Belt and Road Initiative 12; maritime geography of 4, 9; seas 2–4, 7, 10–11, 26, 32, 44, 92; and the 'zone-locked' continental states 4
East China Sea 8, 10, 18, 63, 89
EEZ *see* exclusive economic zone 4, 8–9, 12–17, 20, 25, 34, 55–71, 77, 80–1, 84, 89–90, 92
elevations, low-tide 84, 86

environmental protection 10, 27, 36, 38, 59
Europe 12, 15; and the Middle East 12
exclusive economic zone 31, 34, 57, 59, 61, 70, 81; development of the regime 55–9; disputes 59; excessive claims 58; of foreign countries 57, 61, 66, 69, 92; and freedoms of navigation 71; and hydrographic surveys 63–5; included by the US within the scope of international waters 59–60; and marine scientific research 62–4; and military activities 15, 60–2; and problems with freedoms of navigation in the Asia-Pacific region 69–71; regime 16, 20, 55–6, 59–60, 62, 67, 69, 71, 79, 89, 92–4; and regional issues 67–9; rights 57; surveillance and intelligence collection 15, 61, 66, 66–7, 91; two hundred nautical mile 11; in the Western and Central Pacific 68
Exercise Talisman Sabre 66

Fiji 64
FON *see* freedom of navigation
FONOPs xi, 12, 28, 30, 84–8
freedom of navigation 12, 16–17, 28, 30, 33, 61, 65, 67, 78, 83–9, 92–5; absolute 94; determining availability of high seas 20; development of 13–20; in East Asia 16, 16–20; and EEZ 71; importance of in regional waters 16, 19, 93; and overflight in the South China Sea 17, 30, 56–8, 69, 94

General Provisions on the Adoption, Designation and Substitution of Archipelagic Sea Lanes 39–40
Geneva Convention on Territorial Sea and the Contiguous Zone 25
'global commons' 71
GPASLs *see* General Provisions on the Adoption, Designation and Substitution of Archipelagic Sea Lanes 39–40, 43
'grey areas' in UNCLOS 16, 38, 46–7, 69, 79, 81, 81–2
Gulf of Thailand 6, 8

Hainan 32–4, 66, 68
high seas freedoms 16, 20, 56–7, 59–60, 66, 77, 89; of navigation and overflight 17, 20, 56–7, 59–61, 66, 71; non-resource-related 57; normal 61; of overflight 17
HMS Albion 88
Hong Kong 19, 86, 89
Hornet aircraft 41
hydrographers 39
hydrographic surveys 36, 63–5

IHO *see* International Hydrographic Organization
IMO *see* International Maritime Organisation
incidents 41, 44–6, 66–7, 78, 80–1, 89–90; frequency of 78; major 41, 67; regular 10; risks of 67, 81, 92
INCSEA Agreements 80
Indian Ocean 9, 35, 37, 39–41
Indonesia 2–4, 6, 18, 26, 32, 34, 36–46, 84, 88, 91, 94–5; airspace 41; archipelago 6–7, 9, 29, 35, 39, 41, 45; ASLs 41, 43; claims to have often detected submarines shadowing its naval exercises 46; and the F-16Bs incident 41; proposal to designate three North/South ASLs 39; restrictions on the Portuguese protest vessel entering Indonesian territorial waters 27; sea lanes *40*; sits astride major shipping routes between the Indian and Pacific Oceans 39
Indonesian Government Regulation 37/2002 41, 45
Indonesian Government Regulation No. 37/200296 40
innocent passage 14, 16, 20, 25, 25–30, 37, 39, 41, 46–7, 69, 79, 83, 85, 90, 94; non-suspendable 36; regime 14, 25–6, 28, 30, 41, 45–7, 79; right of 25–7, 32–3, 37, 43, 45–6, 64, 79, 82, 86–7; set out in UNCLOS Article 19(2) 25; of warships 25, 28, 79, 82
Institute of Southeast Asian Studies 6
intelligence collection 17, 58, 61, 66–7, 92
International Hydrographic Organization 65

international law 2, 11–14, 16–17, 26, 55, 58–9, 76, 79, 82, 84, 94–5; and Bernard Oxman's perception of the EEZ in 'quasiterritorial' terms 58; customary 34, 76, 83–4, 92; and politics 94
international lawyers 76, 95
International Maritime Organisation 10, 33, 36, 38–40, 43
international navigation 9, 20, 25, 30, 32–3, 36–41, 43, 45–6, 64, 78, 83, 89, 93
International Regulations for Preventing Collisions at Sea 81
international straits 1, 4, 9–10, 28, 30–5, 38, 47, 89, 93
international waters 9, 59–60, 71
iron ore 19
ISEAS *see* Institute of Southeast Asian Studies
islands 4, 6–8, 10–11, 29, 34, 37, 39, 55, 84–6; artificial 55, 58, 85–6; 'fully entitled' 12; outermost 9, 37

Japan 4, 6, 8–11, 15, 18–19, 29, 32, 35–6, 70, 77, 84, 88–9, 93; archipelago 6–7, 9, 32; and the EEZ 32, 66; government of 36; and plutonium shipments 34; and South Korea 10, 18–19, 34, 77, 80; and the United States 11, 29
Java Sea 8, 41, 94–5
jurisdiction 12–14, 40, 55, 58, 60, 62–3, 67, 70–1, 83–4; claims of 16; extended 15; functional 59; national 55–6, 64, 91; problems concerning 11

Kaplan, Robert 9
Kaye, Stuart 60
Karimata Strait 40
Korean Peninsula 32, 34

language issues (Law of the Sea) 83, 94
law 1–2, 4, 6–7, 14–17, 20, 26, 30, 34, 46, 58–61, 69–70, 76, 78–9, 82–3, 91–5; customary 35, 76, 83, 91–2, 95; and international law 2, 11–14, 16–17, 26, 55, 58–9, 76, 79, 82, 84, 94–5; traditional 92

legal claims 82
legal regimes 56, 62
limitations 25, 56–7, 59, 83, 89, 95; draught 10; major 13
littoral states 8, 10, 35–6, 89, 93
Lombok Strait 9–10, 41, 44
low-tide elevations 84, 86
low-water line 29
Luzon Strait 44, 89–90

Makassar Strait 9–10, 41, 44
Malacca Strait 3, 9–10, 32, 34–7, 44–5
Malacca Strait Council 35–6
Malay Peninsula 6
Malaysia 2–4, 6, 11, 29, 32, 35–7, 61, 86, 91
marine environment 1, 3, 8, 12–14, 33, 36, 43, 55–6, 58, 60, 62–3, 70
marine pollution 4, 35, 43, 93
marine resources 4, 6, 13, 64
marine safety 10, 38
marine sanctuaries 43
marine scientific research 62–4
maritime 36, 38, 55, 59; activities 4, 58; boundaries 6, 10–11, 16, 82; capabilities 3; confidence-building measures 78–80; disasters 43; geography of East Asia 4, *5*, **6**, 9, 16; governance 69; jurisdiction 4, 8, 30, 67, 82; regional forces 4; safety 35; terrorism 35; trade 18–19; user states 1, 25; zones 4, 6, 11–13, 55, 81, 85, 88
maritime powers 1, 27, 45, 56, 63–4; global 92; major 3, 14, 27, 39, 94
maritime security 2–3, 27, 58, 71; arrangements 42; cooperation 37; forces 10, 80
MCBMs *see* maritime confidence-building measures 78–81, 92–5
Memorandum of Understanding on Notification of Major Military Activities Confidence-Building Measures Mechanism 80
Memorandum of Understanding on the Rules of Behaviour for the Safety of Air and Maritime Encounters 80
merchant shipping 3, 16, 47, 86
Mergui Archipelago 7
military activities 15, 60–2; conducting 57, 61, 65, 70; data gathering 65; foreign 92; lawful 60; operations 58, 77; research 69; uninvited 61
Military Maritime Consultative Agreement 69
military surveying 15, 58, 61–3, 65–7, 90; as a form of intelligence collecting 17; and hydrographic surveys 63–5; and survey ships 67
MSC *see* Malacca Strait Council
multilateral agreements 80

nautical charts 65
nautical miles (width of territorial sea) 10, 14, 25, 30, 32, 35, 39, 45, 55, 67, 83, 85–6, 88–9
naval exercises and operations 46, 56, 59, 61, 79
naval vessels 2, 16, 19, 32, 47, 93
navies 77, 80–1, 91; regional 77, 79; structure preferences of different 77
navigation 1–2, 7–8, 10, 12–20, 27–8, 30, 33–6, 40–1, 43–4, 56–61, 65–6, 69–71, 76–9, 82–4, 88–95; aids 33, 36, 93; conditions 45; experts 39; freedoms of 1; information 33; issues 46, 79, 93; limiting of 59; rights of 13, 30, 39, 41, 57, 83–4; safe 36
navigational regimes 14, 16, 20, 25–47, 78, 93, 95; archipelagic sea lanes passage 16, 37–9; and the 'grey areas' 16, 38, 46–7, 69, 79, 81, 81–2; Indonesia 2–4, 6, 18, 26, 32, 34, 36–46, 84, 88, 91, 94–5; and innocent passage 25–30; Malacca and Singapore Straits 35–7; Philippines 42–4
Nicobar Island 67
North Korea 4, 6, 26, 29
Northeast Asia 3, 7, 9–10, 36, 44, 89

Ocean Policy Research Foundation 70, 93
oceans 8, 13, 55, 58–9, 63, 67, 71, 79, 91
oil 9, 12, 34
operations 9, 45, 61–3, 66–8, 77, 80, 84–6, 88; commercial fishing 43; flight 32; littoral 77; military survey 63; oceanographic survey 67; salvage 43

OPRF *see* Ocean Policy Research Foundation
overflight 17, 20, 30, 39–40, 44, 47, 56–61, 66, 69–70, 94; rights of 25, 45; in the South China Sea 17
overseas trade 3, 12, 16, 18–19, 93
Oxman, Bernard 58

Pacific Oceans 6, 9, 37, 39, 41
Paik, Jin Hyun 79
Paracel Islands 7, 11, 29, 84, 86–8
passage 9–10, 14, 26–8, 30–1, 33, 35, 37–8, 43, 45–6, 64, 83, 87, 90; exercising archipelagic sea lanes 41; non-innocent 27–8, 46, 82; regimes 20, 25, 43, 64; regular 13; of shipping 37; submerged 32, 46; suspending 38; unannounced 26
Philippine National Marine Park 43
Philippines 42–4; archipelagic baseline legislation 44; archipelagic waters 6, 43–5; possible archipelagic sea lanes *42*; and South China Sea issues 91
pilots 33
pipelines 56–7, 71
piracy 35
politics 1–2, 20, 94–5; domestic 2, 95; and international law 94
pollution (vessel-source) 14
Port Klang, Malaysia 86
prior notification or authorisation of innocent passage 26–9, 82, 84, 94
problems 27, 58, 71; with freedoms of navigation in the Asia-Pacific region 69–71; with interpreting the general law of the sea as set out in UNCLOS 90; jurisdictional 11; potential 59
protection 14, 56, 58, 60, 93; environmental 10, 27, 36, 38, 59; and preservation of the marine environment 55

Qiongzhou Strait 32, 34

regional countries 1–4, 16, 19, 25–6, 28–9, 58, 66, 69, 71, 77, 93–4
regional guidelines 70
regional issues 67–9
Regional Maritime Security Initiative 37

regional waters 1, 10, 16, 19, 67, 71
regulations 20, 26, 28, 34, 38, 41, 56, 59, 84; concerning activities over which the coastal state legitimately exercises jurisdiction 15; extending 15; on the freedoms of navigation 10; international 34
requirements 25–7, 30, 39, 69, 86, 94; entry 31; pilotage 15; technical 39
research 25, 38, 62, 64, 67, 92, 94; activities 64; historical 82
resources 11, 13, 56, 58–9, 61, 70; offshore 55–6; zones 55, 83
restrictions 2, 14–16, 27, 39, 45, 47, 57, 63, 79, 84, 93; claimed 89, 92; illegal 13; unacceptable 78; unlawful 16; valid 17
rights 13, 17, 19–20, 25, 38, 56–8, 61–2, 70, 78–9, 83, 88, 92; exclusive 71; exercise fishing 15; historic 12; international legal 17; resource-related 12, 56
RMSI *see* Regional Maritime Security Initiative
Rothwell, R. 27
routes 33–4, 37, 39–41, 43, 45, 47, 86, 90; designated 41; direct navigational 9, 27; east-west 41; established shipping 86–7; inter-island shipping 43; international shipping 44; major shipping 32, 37, 39, 43, 89; maritime trade 3
Russia 10, 29, 80

San Bernadino Strait 9
scientific research 8, 13, 15, 17, 55, 58, 60, 62–5, 68, 70
sea lanes 34, 37–9, 41–3; defined 38; designated 40–1, 45; substituting 38
Sea of Japan 8, 10
Sea of Okhotsk 6, 8
seaborne trade 3–4, 88, 93
security 3, 7, 19, 26–8, 35–7, 61, 68, 70, 82, 87, 94; classification 63; energy 3; forces 67, 69; issues 3, 61; national 1, 25, 47, 61, 66; sensitivities 41; treaties 11
Senkaku/Diaoyu dispute 11
Senkaku Islands 10
shipping 2–3, 9–10, 15–16, 35, 43, 47,

89, 93; and aircraft 30–1, 34, 39, 41, 44, 89; amphibious 77; channels 43; coastal Chinese 89; disasters 43; international 9, 33; lanes 91; spy 66, 77; traffic 37, 47, 93; transiting 93
Singapore 2, 4, 6, 9–10, 15, 26, 32, 34–7, 44, 46, 83; and bottleneck shipping 9, 15; and the Indonesian archipelago 7; and sovereignty disputes 10; and the Strait of Malacca 9–10, 18, 32, 35, 35–7, 44, 86
South China Sea 1, 8, 11–12, 17–19, 28–9, 40, 45, 59–60, 68–9, 71, 82, 84–9, 91, 94; and China's claim to the 11; comprises mainly the EEZs of the bordering states 9; issues concerning 91; and the 'militarising' of the 12; northern 11; southern 11; and the sovereignty claims of China, Taiwan and Vietnam over all the Spratly and Paracel islands 11; and Taiwan's claim to the Diaoyu islands 10
South Korea 6, 10, 18–19, 26, 29, 34, 77; and the INCSEA agreement with Russia 80; and Japan 10, 18–19, 34, 77, 80; as a 'middle power' 78; and Taiwan 9
Southeast Asia 9, 41, 43; and the language of the law of the sea 83; and the 'Malacca Dilemma' 3; and Northeast Asia 3; and northern China and Japan 89
sovereign rights 13, 44, 58–9, 61, 67, 94; of coastal states 55; distinguished from sovereignty 59, 94; exercises 59; 'indisputable' 94
sovereignty 11–12, 15, 25, 34, 37, 46, 59, 82–3, 94; claims by China 12; claims by more than one state 8, 11, 87; claims by Vietnam 11; disputes 1, 10–13, 79; distinguished from sovereign rights 59, 94; indisputable 94; offshore 3; state 13
Soviet Union 6, 26–7, 56, 69, 79–80; *see also* Russia
Spratly Islands 6–7, 11–12, 28, 85–6
state control 14–15, 58, 79
state sovereignty 13

states 7–9, 13, 26–31, 34–8, 43, 45–7, 55, 57–65, 67, 70–1, 79–80, 83, 91, 95; EEZ 57–8, 71; foreign 26, 34, 59–60; independent 14; neutral 61
straight baselines 29–30, 33
Strait of Hainan 32
Strait of Malacca 9–10, 32, 35–6, 44–5
strategic tensions 89–90
submarines 4, 6, 16, 25, 31–2, 44–6, 61, 77, 79, 81, 92; and aircraft 4, 61; ballistic missile 7; cables 56–7, 71; operations 45–6, 63, 80; tracking Chinese 68; travelling submerged and transiting 46
Sunda Strait 40
surveillance and intelligence collection 15, 61, 66, 66–7, 91
surveying activities 25, 38, 63–4, 69

Taiwan 4, 6, 9–10, 12–13, 19, 44, 84
Taiwan Strait 9, 13, 89–90
Takeshima islands 10
tensions 14, 18, 69, 78–9, 88, 91; escalating 92; regional 95; strategic 89–90
territorial sea 4, 8–9, 13–14, 20, 25–8, 30–2, 34, 43–6, 55–6, 59, 64, 80–6, 88–90, 92, 94; claiming 32, 88; excessive 86; foreign 63, 79; straight baselines of Vietnam *31*
terrorism 35
THAAD ballistic missile defence system 66
Thailand 4, 6, 8, 19, 29, 61
threats 14–15, 17, 26, 34–5, 61, 83, 91, 93; alleged 17; general 17; possible Chinese 69; potential 25
Timor 8, 10, 41
Torres Strait 10, 33, 35, 76, 78, 93
trade 3, 12, 16, 18–19, 93; crude oil 18; global 19; international 19
trade routes 18–19
trade wars 89
transit 20, 27, 29, 32, 35, 45–6, 79, 83, 90; exercising 44; expeditious 32, 37, 44; of foreign warships 27–9, 45, 85, 90, 94; free 34; mode of 44; publicised 89; unobstructed 37
transit passage 20, 30–5; freedom of 34, 44; hampering 33; principles 38;

transit passage *continued*
   regime 30, 33–5, 37–8, 89–90; rights of 32–4; rules 89
Triton Island 84
Tsugaru Strait 9, 32
Tsushima Strait 9

UN Convention on the Law of the Sea 4, 7–8, 12–16, 25–6, 30, 37–8, 41–3, 45–7, 55–7, 59–64, 67–71, 79, 81–4, 90–1, 95; Articles 7–8, 12, 14–15, 25–9, 32–40, 42, 44, 55–8, 62–4, 66, 85, 87, 89–92, 94; definition of an 'island' 55; enacting 71; navigational regimes 44; Part III 13, 15, 26, 37, 56–7, 59, 61–4, 69–71, 79, 82, 89–90, 95; Part IV 7; Part IX 8, 60; ratified by Thailand in 201, 61; signed by the Philippines 44
UNCLOS *see* UN Convention on the Law of the Sea
United Kingdom 17, 29, 39, 65, 67, 88
United States 6, 8, 10–18, 20, 26–32, 34, 37, 39, 43, 56–63, 65–9, 71, 77–90, 92–5; armed forces 35, 37, 83; claims for freedom of navigation for warships 43; claims to be not taking sides in the sovereignty claims 87; Department of Defense 84; Department of State 57, 84; and the Freedom of Navigation Program 83–5; incident involving aircraft carrier *USS Carl Vinson* 41; intelligence collection aircraft in China's EEZ 41, 66; and Japan 11; Joint Concept for Access and Maneuver in the Global Commons (JAM-GC) 77; Navy 59, 77, 85, 88, 91; ocean surveillance vessel *USNS Impeccable* 66; position on the law of the sea 61; and the Senkaku/Diaoyu dispute 11; submarines 46; THAAD ballistic missile defence system 66; trade considerations 18; warships 13, 86, 88–9
unmanned surface vehicles 92
unmanned underwater vehicles 92
US-China MOU-Rules 81
USNS *Impeccable* 66–8
USS *Carl Vinson* 41
USS *Curtis Wilbur* 84
USS *Guardian* 43
USVs *see* unmanned surface vehicles
UUVs *see* unmanned underwater vehicles

vessels 14, 16, 27, 33, 35, 66–7, 77, 81, 89; electronic intelligence-gathering 66–7; foreign 27; government 70; involving civil law enforcement 81; merchant 41; transiting 47; very large crude carriers 35
Vienna Convention on the Law of Treaties 76
Vietnam 6, 8, 11, 19, 26, 29–33, 82, 84; claims of sovereignty over all the Spratly and Paracel islands 11; government of 30; and the Qiongzhou Strait (Strait of Hainan) 32

warships 16–17, 25–9, 41, 43, 45, 47, 79–80, 82, 85–6, 88, 91, 94; non-innocent passage of 28; sailing without prior notification 86; surface 91; transiting 61, 84
Washington 11–12, 41, 59, 61, 69, 85, 87–8; and the growing strategic tensions with China 90; and operations in the South China Sea 69; and provocations over Beijing 13
waters 7–8, 12, 14, 26, 32, 35–6, 41, 43–6, 60, 63, 65, 77–8, 81, 89, 94; confined 3; disputed 87; internal 25–6, 29–30, 32–4, 43–4, 59; littoral 14, 77; national 83; navigable 81; offshore 55; territorial 27, 47, 81, 90; uncharted 28
West Philippine Sea 8, 82
Western Pacific Naval Symposium 80
Wetar Straits 10, 41
WPNS *see* Western Pacific Naval Symposium

Yellow Sea 6, 8, 66

zones 56–7, 60, 67, 69, 71; contiguous 25, 59, 81, 84–5; metre safety 85; offshore 78